Transport
round the Isle of Man

Steven Dearden and Ken Hassell

When delivered, the Snaefell Mountain Railway cars were probably the most powerful public transport vehicles in the British Isles. A fully laden car weighing some fifteen tons was capable of climbing the 1 in 12 gradient at a steady speed of ten miles per hour. W. A. Camwell photographed car No. 1 passing Dumbell's Row in 1939.

Stenlake Publishing
2001

© Steven Dearden and Ken Hassell 2001
First published in the United Kingdom, 2001,
by Stenlake Publishing, Ochiltree Sawmill, The Lade,
Ochiltree, Ayrshire, KA18 2NX
Telephone / Fax: 01290 423114
www.stenlake.co.uk

ISBN 1 84033 141 0

CONTENTS

The Steam Railway	4
The Manx Electric Railway	21
The Snaefell Mountain Railway	30
Other Tramways and Railways	33
Horse Trams	40
Aviation	46
Shipping	57
Buses	74
Cars and Carriages	88
Motor Car Racing	92
Motorcycle Racing	107

The *Manx Queen* was a common visitor to Douglas in the years prior to 1900. Built in 1881, she had originally been named the *Duchess of Edinburgh* and was intended for the South Eastern Railway's cross-channel service. Unsuitable for this, she was purchased by J. Little and Company of Barrow-in-Furness in 1882 for the Barrow Steam Navigation Company, a partnership between them and the Midland and Furness Railways. The *Manx Queen* sailed on the Douglas to Barrow docks route, and later to Morecambe when Little and Co. retired from the joint undertaking. In 1904 the Midland Railway opened their harbour at Heysham, operating new twin screw steamers. The days of the old paddle steamers had finally passed.

FOREWORD

Situated in the centre of the Irish Sea, the Isle of Man is only 33¼ miles in length with a maximum width of 12½ miles, yet over the years it has boasted a remarkable range of transport systems, many of which survive to be enjoyed by visitors and enthusiasts today.

The beginning of the nineteenth century saw the Island under English administration following the end of hereditary rule by the Stanley and Atholl families. The immediate changes brought about by the 1765 Act of Revestment and later financial settlements were far from beneficial to the islanders, but it was only then that transport links with the Island became an issue. The first important development to open the Island up to visitors was the promotion of a steamship company in 1829, eventually to be known as the Isle of Man Steam Packet Company. The Island was becoming a favourite health resort, and regular communications with England were essential if development was to continue.

At the time there were only three substantial roads: Douglas to Castletown, Douglas to Peel and Castletown to Ramsey. Even these were dangerous for carriages and severely limited the travel opportunities for visitors, whilst also retarding economic development for the local population. The Island was sparsely populated and with the demise of smuggling, farming and fishing were the only significant sources of income. Douglas, however, soon developed into a large modern holiday resort, particularly after the arrival of Governor Henry Brougham Loch in 1863.

For more than 60 years the Red Pier had been the only – and increasingly inadequate – landing facility for visitors. Work on the new Victoria Pier began in 1868 and its opening in 1872 gave impetus to the rapidly growing tourist industry. Improved access to the developing part of the town was needed, and in 1869 a board was set up to plan and build a new main street, Victoria Street, together with a new promenade. Work began in June 1874 and the new Loch Promenade, up to 32 feet seaward of the old shoreline, was opened the following year, providing a continuous roadway round the bay for the first time. The famous horse-drawn Douglas Bay Tramway quickly followed, opening in August 1876. With the development of Douglas, important transport and infrastructure improvements soon began to be made elsewhere across the Island.

Engines No. 7 *Tynwald* and No. 9 *Douglas* wait at Douglas station soon after 1900, prior to the building of the cast iron platform awnings. The signal arm with an 'S' attached allowed a shunting movement to draw ahead past the signal, under control of the signalman. In 1939 *Tynwald* was the first IOMR engine to be taken out of service, having never fully recovering from a serious head-on crash in 1928; today her dismantled remains can be seen at Castletown station. *Douglas*, the last of the smaller engines purchased by the company, was withdrawn in 1953 and is currently in storage.

THE STEAM RAILWAY

Exploiting the great natural beauty of the Island was absolutely essential if the tourist industry was to become a mainstay of the economy. The Isle of Man Railway was the first of the major transport developments on the Island, and the one that contributed most to its development. Proposals to construct a railway dated back as far as 1845, but nothing came of them until 21 April 1870 when a group of local businessmen met to discuss a scheme to build a line from Douglas, initially to the old capital Castletown and later to Port Erin, with lines to Peel and Ramsey to follow. Financial support was slow to emerge and efforts were soon concentrated on the Douglas to Peel line, with help from mainland railway financiers the Duke of Sutherland and John Pender MP.

The 11½ mile long Peel line opened on 1 July 1873 and the 15½ mile Douglas to Port Erin line a year later on 1 August 1874. The lines were a great success, but money remained in short supply and Ramsey still had no railway link. It fell to a separate company, the Manx Northern Railway, to construct the circuitous 16½ mile line from Ramsey to St Johns, where it linked with the IOMR's Douglas to Peel line.

The MNR opened on 23 September 1879, but had an uneasy relationship with the IOMR. In 1899 the electric tramway, which utilised the much more direct east coast route between Douglas and Ramsey, was completed, further threatening the viability of the Manx Northern Railway. The tramway company was interested in taking over the unprofitable MNR, as was the Isle of Man Railway Company. At one point the MNR offered to sell out to the IOMR for £72,500, but this offer was not taken up. It was only after the collapse of Dumbell's Bank in 1900, and the ensuing liquidation of the tramway company that the MNR and its associated Foxdale line company were forced to offer themselves to the IOMR at a reduced price. The Isle of Man Railways Act of 1905 allowed the take-over at a cost of £67,500.

Competition from motor buses began to threaten the railway in the late 1920s, but the IOMR became involved in running buses and set up Isle of Man Road Services in 1930 to coordinate transport operations. This eventually became the mainstay of their business. At the height of operations each of the three main lines carried a dozen trains each way daily during the season. By the 1960s motor cars were posing a real threat to the railway, and decline set in with the number of trains reduced to four or five daily and winter and evening services withdrawn altogether.

Manager A. M. Sheard died at the start of the 1965 season and soon after it became clear that revenue was falling far short of operating costs. In January 1966 the IOMR announced that the railway would not reopen that season. It fell to a new company headed by the Marquis of Ailsa to rescue the service, and the lines reopened as a tourist attraction in June 1967. The timetable was ambitious and losses mounted, with the result that services were reduced in 1968. The last passenger train from Ramsey left on 6 September the same year, and the last train from Peel departed on 7 September. Assisted by the Tourist Board, Lord Ailsa's Isle of Man Victorian Steam Railway Co. kept the Port Erin line open for another three years, with the Isle of Man Railway Company then resuming control to ensure that the Port Erin line reached its centenary in 1974. The railway reached its lowest ebb in 1975 with only four trains daily on the Port Erin to Castletown section, extending to Ballasalla the following year and back to Douglas in 1977. The 1976 general election fortunately returned a government broadly in favour of retaining the Island's vintage transport, and in 1980 all Manx transport systems, except the Douglas horse trams, were united under the control of the Isle of Man Passenger Transport Board.

Visitor numbers continued to fall, but railway and tramway figures held up well thanks to interest from holidaymakers in general and transport enthusiasts in particular. Many special events have been put on over recent years, services and facilities continue to be improved, and the Island's remarkable range of vintage transport systems can now look to the new century with a degree of optimism, assured of their continuing importance to the increasingly specialised Manx tourist industry. We hope you enjoy this photographic collection illustrating some aspects of the Isle of Man's early transport history.

This view of No. 2 locomotive, *Derby*, was taken in front of the Ramsey carriage shed in 1939. *Derby* was one of the original three engines of 1873 and is sadly the only IOMR engine not to survive in some form today. She was fitted with a larger modern boiler in 1923 and remained in service until 1949, but was dismantled and scrapped in 1951. One of the original boilers from Nos. 1–3 was used for some years by the jam factory at Rushen Abbey.

No. 13, *Kissack*, has just arrived under the fine Douglas awning in this inter-war photograph. Named after Edward Thomas Kissack, a director of the railway, she dated from 1910 and was the last of the four larger locomotives to be bought in this period. Although also now in storage, *Kissack* is remembered for maintaining the service with *Loch* between 1971 and 1991.

This serious accident of 22 August 1925 had its origins at Union Mills when the train accidentally left without the guard or brakeman on board after attaching a cattle van in the siding. Warnings were sent to Douglas but the brake on the engine was insufficient to stop the train and, running in cab-first, *Pender* overshot the platform. Fireman William Robinson was killed when he failed to jump clear. As a result of the ensuing enquiry, continuous vacuum brakes began to be fitted to coaches and locomotives.

Engine No. 6, *Peveril*, was closely linked to Peel, spending much of her career on the Peel to Douglas line. As with all the other early engines she received a new, larger boiler prior to 1914 to improve performance with the heavy summer traffic. Her boiler finally gave up in August 1960, and although externally restored she remains inoperative to this day. This picture was taken at Douglas in November 1945.

This unusual photograph of No. 8, *Fenella*, shows her positioned over the pit in the Douglas workshops. It was taken early in her career as regulations later insisted that the walls of the building be whitewashed annually. Delivered in 1894, she was the second engine to be named from Sir Walter Scott's *Peveril of the Peak*, Fenella being the name of the heroine. *Fenella* was withdrawn and put into storage in 1969 after spending most of her time on the Peel and Ramsey lines. The workshops were noted for being able to cope with any job short of constructing a new boiler.

Douglas station could be very busy indeed at the height of the holiday season, as this 1946 photograph illustrates. Petrol remained rationed at the time, and although visitor numbers were slightly down on pre-war figures everyone was determined to enjoy themselves and railway business boomed. Rail traffic was still protected from the full force of road competition by marginally higher bus fares. Passenger numbers at the station peaked in the late afternoon when the Port Erin and combined Peel and Ramsey trains arrived at almost the same time.

Passengers arriving at the station generally walked back to their lodgings, although one family here has acquired one of the popular open-topped hire cars. Kept at 10/-, its pre-war price, the holiday weekly runabout ticket offered great value. The attractive red-brick station buildings were developed over a number of years, the smaller original premises remaining behind the tower to the right.

Leaving Douglas, Port Soderick was the first busy station on the southern line and Ballasalla the second. Ballasalla now has a smart, but rather featureless new building, but the old third class station of 1874 was much more typical of the Isle of Man Railway. There were no platforms but the station had a goods store and two sidings. The passing loop situated here was at the most convenient place for trains to pass, but has now been moved to Castletown because of the proximity of Ballasalla to a level crossing on what is now the busiest road on the Island. The sidings at Ballasalla arose from its importance as a loading point for lime as well as cattle, the latter being transported to and from the now discontinued Tuesday market.

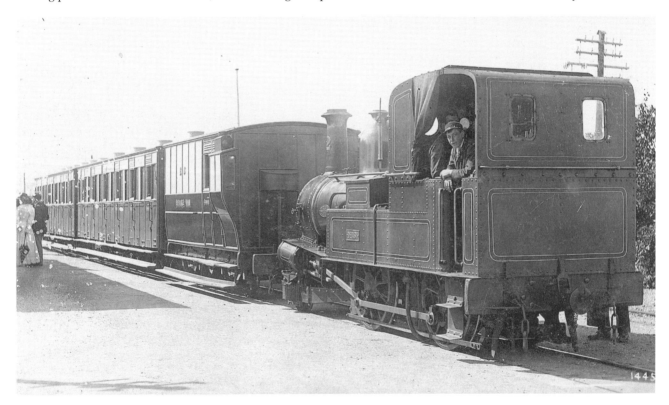

A fine summer day in 1901 and *Derby* waits at Castletown station on her way to Douglas. Note the protruding outlook point on the 1876-vintage brake van E5, in fine condition except for the footboards, which seem somewhat the worse for wear. Double footboards were for use at stations without platforms. The first of the two second class bogie carriages is F1 of 1876, finally burnt out by vandals at St Johns in 1975, the same year that the brake van went for scrap.

In November 1945 Castletown station still had its characteristic large wooden veranda, sadly lost in a recent refurbishment. An interesting array of goods stock can be seen past the goods shed. The station has always been a busy one, but its situation is certainly not central for the town, the railway line having had to make quite a diversion to serve the old capital at all. Traffic levels were still good at this time with the continuing military presence of the RNAS at Ronaldsway, but this was threatened with closure, and another big customer, Castletown Brewery, had recently bought a steam road wagon to reduce the use they made of the railway.

There was originally no formal stopping place at Ballabeg but it seems that in 1876 Flaxney Stowell, a Castletown joiner, was paid to construct the building seen in this 1908 postcard view. This rarely photographed building was later replaced, then the station closed altogether in 1948 – only to be reopened in recent years. It is unlikely that the position of stationmaster here was ever a particularly taxing one.

Port St Mary was another station to have its original building replaced. The small fourth class timber building was replaced in 1898 by this magnificent Ruabon brick structure, second in size only to Douglas. Construction followed strong representation from the ambitious citizens of the village, who were successfully attracting many of the more affluent holidaymakers. It is difficult to believe that it was ever more than a white elephant however. The original 1875 gatekeeper's cottage still survives beyond the station.

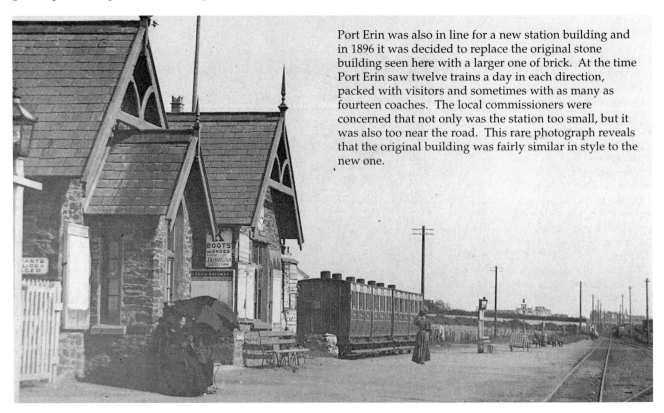

Port Erin was also in line for a new station building and in 1896 it was decided to replace the original stone building seen here with a larger one of brick. At the time Port Erin saw twelve trains a day in each direction, packed with visitors and sometimes with as many as fourteen coaches. The local commissioners were concerned that not only was the station too small, but it was also too near the road. This rare photograph reveals that the original building was fairly similar in style to the new one.

This picture by V. L. Swales gives an idea of the potential size of the Edwardian crowds, with trains carrying over 1,000 passengers being quite amazing for a narrow gauge railway. The old station building was demolished in 1903, at which point the platform was also enlarged and raised. A goods shed followed in 1907, and a new larger locomotive shed the following year. The long, island platform was further extended and extra sidings were added before 1914. The level crossing bisecting the platform is still an unusual feature of Port Erin station today.

Engine No. 12, *Hutchinson*, bought in 1908, was the third new locomotive brought in to operate the newly-acquired Manx Northern line. Rarely out of service, she latterly attracted attention with her controversial dark blue livery (now replaced). H. C. Casserley shows the engine here at Kirk Braddan halt on 2 July 1933 waiting to take visitors back from the once popular open-air Sunday service at old Kirk Braddan. Established in 1897, the halt was only used on Sunday mornings, with extra trains standing by in the hope that the weather would turn wet during the service and persuade people to use the train rather than walk back into Douglas afterwards.

Union Mills station in 1903, looking towards the bridge over the main Douglas to Peel road. Three years later a new siding, cart road, cattle pen and passing loop were added here. The station looks quiet with its small fifth class wood and corrugated iron building, but in fact served the nearby mills, a small quarry and the popular old Douglas racecourse. In later years stationmaster Hogg's beautiful garden displays won the station many a prize.

Crosby was the next station on the Peel line, situated in a secluded spot some way from the main road and centre of the village but busy enough to warrant the building of a more elaborate station building in 1897. The Highway Board had a depot next to the station and this generated goods traffic carrying coal, barrels of tar, and stone chippings – not to mention produce from the streets of Douglas and Ramsey destined for Crosby's infamous manure siding!

Sutherland was the first Isle of Man Railway locomotive and had the honour of pulling the test train from Douglas to Peel on 1 May 1873 and the first official train two months later. She later spent much of her time on the Ramsey line, sharing the Ramsey shed with *Thornhill*, although she is seen here on the branch line at Foxdale. W. A. Camwell's photograph is from May 1939, a time when 'deads' from the disused mine were starting to be taken to form the runway at Jurby's new air force base. The passenger service to Foxdale was suspended later in 1939 and never resumed, but *Sutherland* has been more fortunate, re-emerging from the Port Erin museum and returning to service fully restored in 2000.

No. 3, *Pender*, arrives at Peel in May 1953. *Pender* was the last of the three original engines supplied for the opening of the Peel line in 1873. She was withdrawn from service with a weak boiler in August 1959, and sadly can now only be seen as a sectioned exhibit at the Manchester Museum of Science and Industry. Peel station has also been cleared away although the superior station building, rebuilt in 1907–1908, survives as part of the House of Manannan. A section of line has recently been re-laid to preserve the memory of the railway and keep alive hopes that it could one day be reopened.

Mona was supplied in 1874 along with *Loch* to operate the newly-opened Port Erin line. The new locomotives had larger tanks and bunkers than the first four engines, as the southern line was more steeply banked and required heavier locomotives to operate it (although *Mona* still needed a modified larger boiler in 1914). She is seen here outside Peel's small engine shed in September 1957 in the faded red livery of the period. No. 5 was not the first engine named *Mona* to run on the IOMR, and she shared this name with the locomotive used by contractors constructing the Peel line. *Mona* has been in storage at Douglas since being taken out of service at the end of the 1968 season.

Peel is seen at carnival time in this Edwardian postcard. The two carriages were built by MRCW Saltley in 1875, the 'B' numbered models being a foot shorter than the 'A' type, but still carrying 30 passengers in three plain compartments with few comforts. From 1909 onwards pairs of ex-four wheelers were gradually mounted on new steel bogie underframes and in 1912 B19's body went to coach F64 and its chassis to G15, while B1's body went to carriage F62 in 1926.

Waterfall halt was the only intermediate station on the Foxdale line, serving Lower Foxdale village and the nearby Hamilton waterfall, once a popular tourist attraction. The original station building had been removed by 1905 and this photograph by H. C. Casserley, dating from July 1933, shows the replacement – actually no more than a temporary timber office from St Johns. Passenger services on the line ceased in 1939 but Waterfall actually saw its busiest period in 1944 when it was used as a base for night-time army exercises.

Magnificent coastal views were a feature of the line from Peel to Kirk Michael, the track generally being on an embankment raised well above the road. Glen Mooar was crossed by a wrought iron lattice viaduct of three 60-foot spans, with the rails a full 75 feet above the river bed. The original structure became weak and was replaced by one of steel in 1921 following many years of weight and speed restrictions.

Kirk Michael's fine stone-built station is typical of the Manx Northern Railway and survives today as the village fire station. The original goods shed, to the left, was replaced in 1923, the line being extended through it into a carriage siding. This was to accommodate excursions to nearby Glen Wyllin, with trains sometimes starting and terminating here at the height of the glen's popularity.

A typical road crossing on the railway to the north of Peel in about 1905. The job of gatekeeper proved to be a dangerous one over the years, with more than one employee killed by passing trains. Gatekeepers would often be retired railwaymen or the wives of employees, the position frequently being accompanied by a small cottage for Manx Northern Railway employees (although the Isle of Man Railway usually only provided a sentry-box type hut). Gates on particularly quiet roads could normally be left closed against road traffic at this time.

A second photograph of *Peveril* (see also page 6) shows her passing St Germain's station on the 3.45 p.m. Douglas to Ramsey service of 9 September 1957. St Germain's was improved that year, the station house being leased and supplied with electricity for the first time. It had been another disappointing year, however, with industrial unrest on the mainland and poor weather affecting visitor – and hence passenger – numbers. The Ramsey to Peel bus service had even been reduced in an attempt to encourage rail traffic.

Ballaugh station was a typically well-built Manx Northern structure of Peel sandstone. The main stop between Kirk Michael and Ramsey, it also had a passing loop, with trains occasionally changing engines here. There was a goods yard too, and the stone goods shed can still be seen near the road today.

Sulby Glen station is seen here in 1938 with its short, raised platform which could only accommodate three carriages. The original station had been modified in 1880 and was demolished and replaced in 1910. This was because its construction had only been authorised at a late stage in the line's development and it had accidentally been sited too close to the track. Its successor was an unusual building, with the large awning forming an integral part of the station roof. A goods store at the end of the platform was one of the last MNR timber buildings to survive.

Sulby Glen marked the last summit on the line to Ramsey and the track then fell away to Sulby Bridge station, only three-quarters of a mile and three minutes' journey further on. A quieter station, it had a more typical MNR building of red Peel sandstone, surviving today as a private residence. This photograph dates from August 1959, a warmer summer than the previous few and one that brought better passenger figures, although discussions about the line's future were already taking place and the outlook was not good.

The faded grandeur of Ramsey station, seen here looking towards Bowring Road in the 1960s. A timber canopy covered the platform and openings led to the booking hall, waiting room, stationmaster's office and an old news kiosk long used as a store room. The station had once housed the offices of the Northern company and a grand refreshment room, but latterly always seemed to be nearly deserted.

All the IOMR engines were Beyer–Peacocks, but the Manx Northern Railway also owned one engine made by the company. *Thornhill* dated from 1880 and was named after the Ramsey residence of the company's chairman J. T. Clucas. After the takeover by the Isle of Man Railway

Thornhill enjoyed a long working life on the Ramsey and Peel lines, finally being withdrawn in 1963 with a defective boiler. Seen here at Ramsey in the early years of IOMR ownership, the most obvious difference to the other engines is her lack of chimney numerals. Left in poor condition by the MNR, she was overhauled in 1910 and fitted with a spare boiler from *Loch*. She was allocated the number 14 at the same time, but this was only added to her livery when *Thornhill* received a brand new boiler in 1921.

The carriage featured in this November 1945 photograph taken at Douglas is F24, a Saltney bogie brake composite of 1896. Some carriages of this type were supplied with open construction for third class use rather than partitioned compartments, but F24 came with five compartments, four originally designated first class. The number of third class sections was increased from one to three in 1929, reflecting changes in passenger preferences. Some carriages of this type still form part of the current rolling stock, but F24 was a victim of the 1975 St Johns shed fire.

Larger and more powerful than all the other engines, *Mannin*, delivered in March 1926, was the last Beyer–Peacock locomotive to be purchased by the railway. During busy summer periods many trains on the Douglas to Port Erin line had previously had to be double-headed, partly because all the four-wheeled type of carriages were now on heavier bogie underframes. *Mannin* was therefore a useful economy measure, spending most of her career on the southern line out-stationed at Port Erin. She is pictured here at Douglas in 1957, seven years before her withdrawal and eventual placement in the Port Erin railway museum.

THE MANX ELECTRIC RAILWAY

The Manx Electric Railway grew from a plan to construct a road from the Derby Castle end of Douglas promenade to Ramsey. A scheme to build a 3-foot gauge railway along the route was included in the agreement, with capital being raised by the promoter Alexander Bruce. A single line of track had been completed as far as Groudle by September 1893, and the service opened for the last few days of the season. This famous photograph shows car 3 and trailer 16 on test above Groudle prior to the opening of the line.

The potential year-round value of the railway was quickly proved during the 'Big Snow' of February 1895. The roads and steam railway line to Ramsey were cut off for days, but the electric line was quickly cleared to the Laxey terminus. The mails for Ramsey were transported to Laxey and then carried the rest of the way on the postmen's backs. This picture of car 9 shows the original Hopkinson bow collector overhead equipment. This proved unreliable, and in 1897 a decision was taken to re-equip the entire line for trolley pole operation using the familiar fixed head type of trolley wheel.

Car 5 came from the same batch as No. 9, arriving in time for the opening of the extension to Laxey and the start of the year-round service in 1894. Built by G. F. Milnes, these cars featured platform vestibules more suited to a Manx winter. With minor modifications, including the first windscreen wipers to be fitted in the fleet, car 5 remains in service today. By the time this early photograph was taken, the original unsprung bow collectors had been replaced by a sprung type, but these were still unreliable and here an accident has taken place just out from Groudle. (David Bailey collection.)

The line finally reached Ramsey Palace terminus in July 1899 where trailer 44 is shown with a power car still in the original livery. Trailers 44–48 were new in 1899 and were only fitted with side roller shutters after 1903. The other trailers from this class remain in service, but No. 44 was unfortunately lost in the serious 1930 Laxey depot fire. The temporary station building at Ballure was transported to Ramsey for the opening of the line, and other staff facilities were provided in the concert hall, which was only sold off by the company in 1938.

The four power cars delivered in 1895 were only in service for a short period, being withdrawn from passenger service in 1902 to re-emerge as goods vehicles. They were vestibuled saloons seating 48, very similar to the Snaefell cars, which were also initially supplied without saloon windows and clerestories. They also lacked the usual glazed end doors, instead having a wrought iron gate across the top of the steps. This early view of trailer 20 at Groudle is another rarity, as the 1894 trailers 17–22 were renumbered 34–39 as early as 1898. (David Bailey collection.)

One of the renumbered trailers, No. 37, waits at Groudle accompanied by a winter saloon in about 1920. No. 37 survived the 1930 Laxey fire and is the only trailer of its class to occasionally still be seen in service. The fine Groudle Glen Hotel building has recently been restored to immaculate condition.

In 1899 G. F. Milnes supplied four fully-glazed and vestibuled 'winter' saloons with transverse seating for 48 passengers. They remain the largest cars in the fleet and have served almost continuously each summer and winter since introduction, their mileages having passed 1 million per car. No. 20 is in the idyllic surroundings of Laxey station in 1939, a view that remains almost unchanged today. The presence of advertising boards on Snaefell car 1 is perhaps the most significant difference.

Another one of W. A. Camwell's classic photographs shows converted crossbench trailer No. 25 with trailer 43. The formation of the Manx Electric Railway Company in 1902 led to a programme of upgrading, including the motorisation of the four former trailers Nos. 24–27. This converted class of cars earned the nickname 'paddleboxes' because of the uneven configuration of their footboards, which resulted from the fitting of wider Brush trucks at this time.

This Edwardian photograph and the following one both show Laxey station with trailer cars that were destroyed in the 1930 Laxey depot fire. Trailer 38 was one of a batch of six delivered from G. F. Milnes in 1894. These had more substantial fixed roofs and boarded end bulkheads. Only two of these cars, 36 and 37, survived the fire.

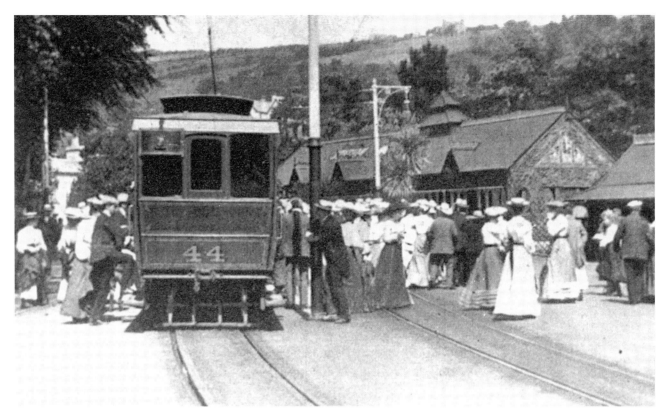

Cars 44–48 arrived for the opening of the Ramsey extension in 1899, when extra trailers were required for the expanded service and to redress the imbalance created by the conversion of some trailers to motor cars. No. 44 was the only one of the batch lost in the 1930 fire; the others are still in regular use.

The final additions to the MER's fleet of motor cars were crossbench cars Nos. 32 and 33, built by UEC Preston in 1906. They were the most powerful cars in the fleet, and track condition allowing, could do a return journey from Douglas to Ramsey in well under two hours. They are still in regular use today, although 75 minutes each way would be the usual journey time now. Trailer 47, seen here by the Mines Tavern, is from the 1899 G. F. Milnes delivery.

An Edwardian view of the Douglas terminus showing the much-missed Derby Castle and the great tramway canopy, still complete with clock tower. The weather could have been better, but the spectacular line-up of motor cars and trailers here suggests the expectation of a good day's business at the height of the summer season.

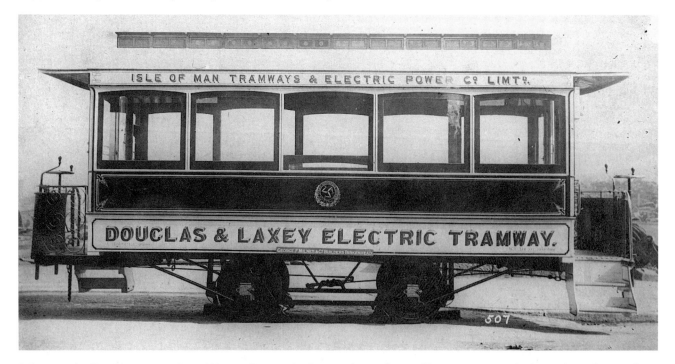

Saloon trailer No. 59 originated in 1899 as a directors' saloon and was the smallest passenger vehicle on the railway. This manufacturer's photograph shows it in its original state mounted on four-wheel trunnion gear. It seemingly ran very badly and was quickly mounted on spare bogies in 1900, although it still saw little use except for transporting King Edward VII and Queen Alexandra back to Ramsey from Douglas in August 1902.

In 1933 the platform entrances of trailer 59 were transposed to coincide with those of the power cars, and with later modifications to improve running this allowed the trailer to be used more regularly on special occasions. One such occasion was the visit of members of the Light Railway Transport League in May 1955. Car 1 (now the oldest operating electric tramcar in the world) hauled No. 59 and was followed by toastrack motor No. 32, with the party seen here at Dhoon Quarry. When not in use, No. 59 is on display in the small museum at Ramsey.

In later years the only goods stock to be seen tended to be small closed vans or the large mail van, the remainder having fallen into disuse after a period of heavy wartime usage transporting stone waste from Laxey for use in airport construction. A mail van would be attached to the 10 a.m. and 8 p.m. Douglas to Ramsey workings and the 6.45 a.m. and 2.30 p.m. Ramsey to Douglas cars. Here winter saloon No. 22 is shown pulling a mail van on the approach to Ballaglass Glen in the inter-war period.

From 1903 MER conductors acted as auxiliary postmen (for no extra payment), emptying the eight lineside letter boxes. The first out from Ramsey was at Belle Vue, being emptied here in 1955 by conductor Mr Sanderson. Mail collections continued right to the end of the year-round service in 1975.

Saloon car No. 6 approaches Queen's Drive in July 1966, still the first possible stop out of Ramsey at the time. Delivered new in 1894 for the expanded year-round service, No. 6 still has its original longitudinal seating but with a central partition that has reduced seating capacity to only 32. All the cars in this class have since lost the twin end windows that can be seen here.

Rather greater changes can be seen in this 1905 view of Queen's Drive, when the halt merited its own shelter. The winter saloon is in the 1904 livery, now reading 'Douglas, Laxey & Ramsey Electric Railway' rather than 'Tramway', and is pulling one of the open goods wagons (the transporting of sheep and other livestock continued into the 1920s). Note that the town's bathing huts have now been relegated to use on these allotments.

Trailers 40–43 were built by G. F. Milnes in 1903, numbers 40 and 41 being amongst those lost in the Laxey depot fire. The seven burnt trailers were replaced by only three new English Electric trailers, the newest vehicles in the MER fleet. They were virtually identical to the burnt cars right down to the acutely curved side pillars that had originally caused difficulties when roller blinds had been fitted. No. 40 is shown here at the back of the Ramsey Plaza in the 1950s. This was a period of decline, reflected in the simplified livery of the time; the MER was only saved by Tynwald nationalising the line in November 1956.

THE SNAEFELL MOUNTAIN RAILWAY

When the electric tramway reached Laxey in 1894 the idea of a railway to the summit of Snaefell – at 2,034 feet the Island's only mountain – suddenly seemed a realistic possibility. The Snaefell Mountain Railway Association first met on 4 January 1895 and amazingly the line opened for service the same August. A shelf had to be cut into the solid rock for much of the distance and the achievement was all the more remarkable given the pioneering nature of the technology. The track, with its central Fell rail for safety, was unique in the British Isles. Six 46-seat bogie passenger cars were delivered by G. F. Milnes and No. 6 is seen here in about 1905 with a group of motormen and conductors.

The original station for the Snaefell line was inconveniently sited up by the current depot building. In 1897 it was moved to this short-lived location just to the west of what is now the main road; the familiar joint Laxey station opened the following year. Cars 2 and 3 can be seen here with the extra Fell rail also clearly visible.

8156. I.o M/Laxey. Snaefell Mountain Riy. G.N.

Another car in the original Snaefell Mountain Tramway red and white livery and varnished teak trim, but dated to 1900 or later by the presence of one of the large rooftop advertising boards. The trams were quickly fitted with sliding windows in place of the original canvas blinds, and roof clerestories were installed over the winter of 1896–1897. The fine Station Hotel refreshment rooms at Laxey were destroyed by fire on 24 September 1917.

A second view of car No. 2 (see opposite) taken over twenty years later in 1919, by which time she was painted in red livery and bearing an advertising board. The original wooden Snaefell Summit station and Terminal Hotel had proved unsuitable for the large number of passengers carried, and a new combined station and hotel building was opened in 1906. The impressive castellated structure, devastated by fire in 1982, was kept busy catering for the popular full-day tours to Sulby Glen offered by the railway company in the inter-war years.

Although the Snaefell line closed on 20 September 1939 and didn't reopen until 1946, No. 5 was used quite frequently during this period to transport workers from the internment camps on the Island to the Bungalow, where they were occupied in digging peat for winter fuel. They are seen here on 5 April 1943. (David Bailey collection.)

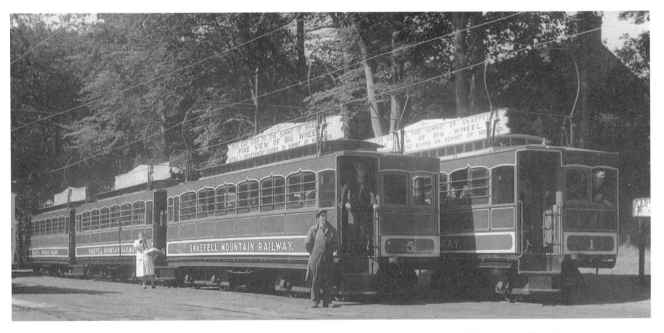

A rarely seen line-up of all six cars, early on a summer day in the 1950s. As time passed the cars suffered from an increasing number of embarrassing motor failures, and in 1977 new trucks and roof-mounted control gear, largely obtained from a batch of ex-Aachen tramcars, were fitted to ensure the line's survival. Car 5 suffered a more drastic fate when she was burnt out in a disastrous fire at the summit on 16 August 1970. She was rebuilt with modern windows and seating, and without the familiar clerestory.

OTHER TRAMWAYS AND RAILWAYS

The only pier tramway on the Island was that on the Queen's Pier, Ramsey. In the early 1900s steamers from Belfast, Whitehaven, Liverpool and Ardrossan all called here and ten men were employed to transport passenger luggage and cargo. Despite plans to electrify the line, however, the rolling stock all remained hand-propelled until a petrol-driven Planet locomotive was delivered in 1937. The Planet is seen here in 1950, two years before a Wickham railcar was added to the passenger stock.

The Wickham railcar displays the 1956 fare structure in this photograph (the original 1899 hand-propelled car can be seen in the siding to the right). The last tram ran on the pier on 9 September 1981, the Harbour Board having passed its running on to several private operators by then. The Planet engine and trailer survive, as does the track, but there are currently no plans to put the line back into service again. The railcar helped on the old Ramsey to Peel steam railway line when the rails were being lifted in 1974 but was unfortunately later scrapped.

The development of Groudle Glen as a pleasure resort and the arrival of the Manx Electric Railway encouraged the idea of a small gauge railway to link the diverse attractions within the glen. Work began in 1895 and the three-quarter mile long 2-foot gauge steam railway was an immediate success when it opened on 20 July 1896. The zoo near the mouth of the glen was the biggest attraction and the first steam engine was appropriately named *Sea Lion*. Seen here at Lhen Coan, Bamforth's photograph also gives a detailed view of one of the original passenger coaches.

A second locomotive, *Polar Bear*, arrived with four additional coaches in May 1905. Easily identified by her square (as opposed to round) cab windows, she is seen here at Sea Lion Rocks in about 1935. *Polar Bear* left the Island in 1967, initially for the Brockham Museum in Surrey, although she made a brief return visit to the glen in recent years.

The high price of coal after 1918 encouraged the owners to order two battery-electric locomotives in 1921. One was involved in an accident soon after delivery, and generally the new engines were never a success, being withdrawn after only six years when the original steam locomotives were brought out of retirement. This picture shows one of the battery engines (which were also called *Sea Lion* and *Polar Bear*) at Sea Lion Rocks, with the entrance to the zoo to the right.

Following the Second World War, the railway reopened in 1950 but *Sea Lion* was unable to re-enter service and business was not good. Closure followed after the 1958 season, with the line reopening in 1961–1962 after which the rails were removed and the buildings demolished. This photograph shows the remains of *Sea Lion* after removal to the Kirk Michael Steam Centre in 1968. Plans to restore the railway were announced in 1982, and thanks to the voluntary efforts of members of the Isle of Man Steam Railway Supporters Association, the first passengers were carried on the partly restored line the following year. A rebuilt *Sea Lion* was amazingly in steam at Groudle again in 1987, 48 years after her last use. Today the fully-restored line is once again Groudle's biggest attraction.

The most popular way to reach the attractions of Douglas Head and the Marine Drive was to take one of the attractive double-ended, quadruple screw ferries from the Victoria Pier to the Battery Pier. As well as the *Rose* (pictured on the back cover), the Douglas Steam Ferry Company operated two other vessels – the *Shamrock* and the *Thistle* (the latter is seen here minus her funnel and some of her low bench seating). Originally owned by Lawrence Boni and later by R. Knox, the ferries finally succumbed to competition from a new bus service to the Head. The paddle steamers in the background of this picture are the *Mona III* and *Ben-my-Chree II*, dating the photograph to before 1906.

Once across the harbour, holidaymakers could take the Douglas Head Incline Railway from near Port Skillion. This opened in 1900, and a combined 2/- return ticket for the ferry, incline railway, tramway, and Port Soderick funicular could be purchased at the Victoria Arcade office. The four-foot gauge incline railway had two cars built by Hurst Nelson, and was operated by an oil-powered engine at the top of the line. The incline railway outlasted the ferry, closing in 1953 when it was dismantled.

Another little-known 'railway' feature of Douglas Head at the turn of the century was this scenic railway built on wooden trestles and known as 'Bob's Coaster'. It never seems to feature in postcard views, and would appear to have been lost in the disastrous fire of 28 August 1900 when the 200 foot Warwick Tower was destroyed along with its pavilion and sideshows.

Taking visitors from the Head to Port Soderick, the Douglas Southern Electric Tramway was the only standard gauge electric tramway on the Island, and was particularly notable for the scale of the civil engineering work it entailed. This was carried out by Heenan and Froude, builders of Blackpool Tower. Today only the entrance gates to the Marine Drive remain, seen here in about 1905 with a packed car No. 1 passing through. The notice on the archway gives an important warning: 'Keep your seats passing through arch, don't touch the overhead wire'. The turnstile to the right was for pedestrians who had to pay 2d for entry as opposed to 6d each way for the tram ride.

This W. A. Camwell photograph shows tramcars Nos. 1 and 7 with inspector Mr Colquitt at the Douglas Head terminus in May 1939, the last year of operation. The discs with number 4 on them indicate that four cars were in service, a reminder on the single line tramway that cars should wait to pass each other at the designated passing loops displaying a '4'. The system was introduced as a result of the only accident in the history of the line in 1909. The Steam Packet vessel is the *Tynwald IV* of 1936.

Taken on the same day in 1939 as the previous picture, this photograph shows car No. 1 approaching Port Soderick. An unusual feature of the trams was that both front and rear staircases were on the landward side, a necessary safety measure given how closely the line hugged the cliffs along its four mile length. The line carried an average of over 222,000 passengers a year, although latterly numbers dwindled and the trailer cars were rarely needed.

Car No. 2 arrives at the Port Soderick terminus in 1938. Port Soderick was once so popular that it was not only served by launches from Douglas and the trams, but the steam railway often had to lay on specials or extra carriages banked by a second engine to cope with the traffic. The Southern Electric Tramway had originally opened as far as the Whing on 7 August 1896 (just before the opening of the cable tramway), although bridgework delayed the opening to Port Soderick terminus until 1 April 1897. Cars 1–6 were the original 1896 motor cars although trailers 7 and 8 were later converted to motor use too.

Once Port Soderick was reached, yet another funicular railway could be taken down to the attractions on the beach, although the 150-step ascent made the return journey even more attractive. Erected by the Forrester family, the railway opened in July 1898 using equipment which was purchased from the Falcon Cliff site in Douglas where it had operated since 1887 (although the Port Soderick line was substantially longer). New cars were purchased and the originals can be seen here in use as kiosks on the promenade. The whole complex, including the Port Soderick Hotel, was sold in 1947 and the cliff lift was dismantled, with only the stone pillars remaining today.

A curious variant on the cliff lift existed for many years at the Cunningham Holiday Camp. This took the form of a 160-foot escalator, starting from the castellated entrance still to be seen in Switzerland Road, Douglas. The escalator is shown here as installed in 1923, although it was doubled in width in 1938. Campers rode free of charge (the wooden chairs were for 'up' only), and the more energetic could race the passengers along the adjoining staircase. The parallel steel chain-link belt with its continuous line of seats was powered by electric motors and remained in use into the 1960s.

HORSE TRAMS

Thomas Lightfoot, a retired civil engineer, quickly saw the possibilities of a horse tramway along the new Douglas promenade, lodging plans as early as November 1875 and commencing construction the next June. The track ran close to the sea wall for much of its length but was placed centrally here on the Loch Promenade. Initially comprising a single track with passing places, the tramway starting to carry the public on 7 August 1876. The last section to be completed ran from the Iron Pier to the foot of Victoria Pier, with authorisation to open the complete track granted on 31 January 1877 after the road had been raised to the level of the track. This rare photograph shows material being added to the road to raise it.

We tend to think of the horse trams as a summer service run primarily for the visitors, but this photograph of the 'Big Snow' of February 1895, with a winter saloon waiting at the left, shows that this was not always the case. The Highway Board hired large numbers of the Island's unemployed to restore vital communication links following the heavy snowfall. Operating only on weekdays and for a 1d fare rather than the 2d summer rate, the winter service continued until it was replaced by motor buses in 1927.

This photograph shows the more familiar set-up after 1889 with the ubiquitous Jubilee Clock and the tramway operating on a double track. Thomas Lightfoot ran into financial difficulties in 1882 when ownership passed to Isle of Man Tramways Ltd., with Douglas Corporation taking over the running of the line in 1902. The double-decker car is one of Nos. 2–4, which had arched tops to the saloon windows. It is advertising Injebreck Pleasure Gardens, a popular resort prior to the completion of Douglas's new reservoir there in 1905. To the left of the clock, behind the shoeshine men, one of the upper Douglas horse buses that operated until the opening of the Upper Douglas Cable Tramway in 1896 can be seen.

This photograph was taken on a summer morning in about 1903, and the three cars illustrate the frequency of the seasonal service. Two of them are eight-bench open toastracks. No. 31 was delivered new in 1894 and survived until 1987 when it was broken up, having serving as a training car for several years. The tram in the centre, No. 34, dates from 1896 and still survives. This was one of a batch of six similar G. F. Milnes cars, the sunshade-roofed crossbench model being a new type for Douglas and incorporating many new features including the brass grab rails seen here. In the foreground a cable car waits at the Jubilee Clock terminus.

Double-decker tram No. 3 was one of the first to arrive in Douglas, and was manufactured by the Starbuck Car and Wagon Co. Ltd. in 1876. Alterations, which included the fitting of a more robust quarter-turn staircase, eventually increased capacity to 36. Roller bearings were fitted to improve running in 1934 and Nos. 2 and 3 remained in service until 1948, being scrapped the following winter. The open toastracks increased their capacity by having additional passenger seats on the driver's platform, a popular vantage point, if something of a distraction.

No. 33, another of the 1896 roofed crossbench trams built by G. F. Milnes, rounds the curve by the old promenade shelter. This was the last section of the track to be doubled, and followed the demolition of the old lifeboat house and the widening of Colonel's Walk by 11 feet to form the Harris Promenade. Work began to improve this dangerous section of the twenty minute journey at the end of 1895, although afterwards the curve was still very pronounced and gave a blind corner at busy periods, even if speeds were only 7–9 mph.

The level track and light traffic meant that the Douglas tram horses had an easier job than most, but public opinion initially put pressure on Thomas Lightfoot to use two horses on the double-decker trams. The original primitive spiral staircases also proved difficult for ladies to negotiate in the fashions of the time, although close inspection of the double-decker tram in this picture (with a later quarter-turn staircase), reveals a full complement of ladies on top, their ankles concealed by the dual purpose advertising boards. The nearer tram is one of Milnes' roofed crossbench cars of 1896.

A 1950s photograph depicting one of the convertible all-weather cars obtained from the Vulcan Motor and Engineering Co. Ltd. of Southport in 1935. The process of converting the car from crossbench to saloon style was a particularly ingenious one, but by 1969 these cars only operated as 27-seat saloons as their age made the conversion increasingly time-consuming. No. 50 was broken up in 1982, but No. 49 survives in storage at Douglas. The Douglas Corporation bus is an AEC Regent Mk III of 1948, which survived in the National Transport fleet until 1977.

Two open 'toastracks', the type of car most people associate with the horse trams, cross in this 1920s photograph. Seating 32 on eight crossbenches, they were almost equal in capacity to the double-deckers but with the advantage of being much lighter to pull. The elegant curved iron arches supported carriage lamps, which were very important bearing in mind that on summer services the last car left the Victoria Pier at 11.20 p.m. Battery lighting was introduced from 1933 and the last oil lamps were removed from cars soon after services resumed in 1946. The cars of the day were advertising sheet music for popular songs published by Lawrence Wright.

Car 27 was one of the three elegant winter saloons delivered in 1892. Only the body is seen here, displayed outside the depot on the occasion of the visit of members of the Light Railway Transport League in 1956. Platform vestibules were added in 1895, increasing seating capacity to 30. Although the saloons were intended for the now discontinued winter service, all survive in regular use today whenever the weather is threatening.

The Douglas cable tramway opened on 15 August 1896 and started at the Jubilee Clock, travelling up Victoria Street and Prospect Hill to Bucks Road, Woodbourne Road, York Road and (originally) back down to the promenade at Broadway. The route was cut back to Stanley View in 1902. Photographs taken at locations other than the Jubilee Clock are scarce, but this view shows No. 77, one of the original crossbench cars (rebuilt as a saloon in 1903–1904) passing the House of Keys in 1914. The line was finally closed and replaced by motor buses on 19 August 1929.

A cable car waits in the distance at its kerbside terminus in Stanley View in this 1926 picture. By this time the system was being used less and had become noted for its noisiness as the track, cable and pulleys wore out. The rattling of the windows in the enclosed saloon cars earned them the local nickname of 'Devils', and when services finally came to an end it was noted 'what a strange, quiet place Douglas has become'.

AVIATION

The first aircraft ever to visit the Isle of Man were Claude Graham-White's Farman biplane and George Barnes's Bleriot monoplane, both of which arrived in July 1911. The monoplane was unfortunately damaged on arrival, although conditions on Tynwald Day were unsuitable for the proposed race around the Island against the Steam Packet's fastest vessel, the *Ben-my-Chree*, anyway. After much delay, however, Graham-White did take off at 4.40 p.m., circling the ship as she set off around the Island before returning to his aerodrome at Noble's Park. Three hours later he escorted the vessel back into port and gave a more exciting display of aerobatics for the patiently waiting crowds.

July 1914 saw the first seaplane to visit the Island, an Avro 504 converted to land and take off on water by the attachment of floats on a tubular frame. The Avro was piloted by a Mr Raynham and offered pleasure flights during Douglas carnival week along with a Bleriot machine flown by a Mr Salmet. Free flights were awarded to lucky coupon holders and the attraction was the highlight of the season.

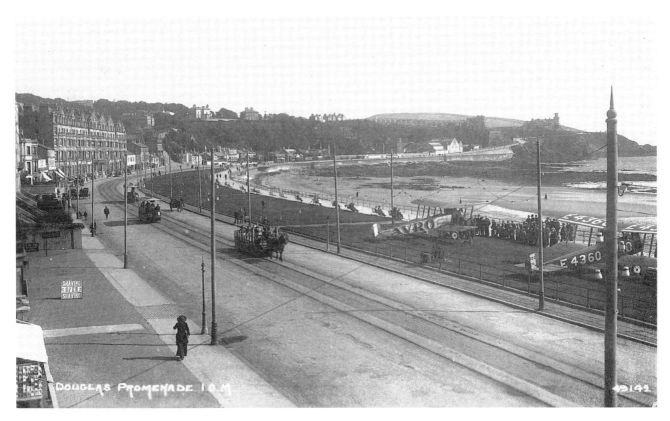

A. V. Roe & Co. Ltd. of Manchester repurchased a large number of their Avro 504s at the end of the First World War and put them to work at holiday resorts throughout the country. The war had aroused a lot of public interest in flying, and business was brisk despite the relatively high cost, with prices starting at one guinea. A section of Douglas beach was designated as a landing ground and the aircraft were allowed to use the grassy section of the adjoining promenade when they were not in use.

Interest was generated by giving free publicity flights for local celebrities such as the mayor and music hall artiste Florrie Ford. Dowty's have photographed the original aircraft, Lieutenant G. B. Moxon's Avro No. 2, which retained its military serial number throughout its stay in Douglas. A second aircraft arrived in August, and occasional flights were also offered from Ramsey.

The International Aviation Co. of Liverpool offered flights the following year (1920), but complaints from hoteliers and deckchair operators meant that no further concessions were granted. The two pilots were Lieut. J. Rimmer and Lieut. George Hughes, and this postcard was specially produced to present to passengers after their flight around the bay.

International Aviation Co.

"Dowty"
Copyright.

Flight Lieutenant R. H. C. Monk played an important role in Manx aviation history. Charter trips from Blackpool made him a regular visitor to the Island and in 1932 he established British Amphibious Air Lines to operate a regular evening service to Douglas, the idea being that at this time of day the bay would be clear of most of the pleasure craft. A Saro Cutty Sark amphibian named *Progress I* was purchased and an incident-free service operated over the summers of 1932 and 1933, using Derbyhaven or Ronaldsway if the waters were too rough in Douglas bay. One of the flying boat's propellers can be seen on display in the restaurant at Ronaldsway Airport.

When Blackpool and West Coast Air Services first started to use Ronaldsway Aerodrome in 1933 there were only a couple of storage huts on the site and passengers gathered in the nearby Derbyhaven Hotel. A wooden terminal building was constructed and shared with the rival Manx Airway run by Railway Air Services. This postcard was submitted in March 1940, and perhaps surprisingly was passed for publication by the wartime Press and Censorship Bureau.

One of West Coast Air Services' de Havilland DH84 Dragons is shown here on the Blackpool to Isle of Man service. A six passenger layout was normal, but this could be increased to nine or ten on occasion. Traffic proved insufficient for two rival operators and amalgamation led to the formation of Isle of Man Air Services in September 1937.

HALL CAINE AERODROME, RAMSEY, I.O.M.   R.329.

The Hall Caine aerodrome at Close Lake on the road between Ramsey and St Judes was only in use for four years from 1935, with scheduled services ending as early as September 1937. It had briefly been very busy with United Airways operating to Blackpool four times daily and three times per week to Belfast. Northern and Scottish introduced a service to Renfrew and Carlisle with services to Liverpool and London following. After two successful years, however, when over 10,000 passengers were carried, a number of company changes led to Ronaldsway being favoured and a decline set in.

Used as a military airfield from the outbreak of war, Ronaldsway was commissioned as HMS *Urley* on 21 June 1944. 'Urley' is Manx for eagle and the badge echoes the legend of an heir to the house of Derby being found in an eagle's nest as a baby. As a Royal Navy air station, HMS *Urley* trained crews in methods of torpedo attacks, anti-submarine warfare and dive-bombing.

The main aircraft used was the Fairey Barracuda, a high-wing monoplane with Rolls Royce Merlin engines carrying a crew of three: pilot, observer/gunner and wireless operator. The aircraft based at Ronaldsway were operated by three second line squadrons – 747, 713 and 710 – with Barracudas making up 92 of the 120 aircraft on station.

A Fairey Barracuda with wings prepared for folding (the wings folded so that the plane could be loaded onto an aircraft carrier). The Barracuda had a distinctly odd appearance and was dogged throughout its career by virtue of being overweight. Strengthening of the airframe and the fitting of additional equipment played havoc with the aircraft's take-off and climbing performance. It certainly made its mark, however, when 42 aircraft dive-bombed and badly damaged the German battleship *Tirpitz* in April 1944, although most squadrons were disbanded or re-equipped with other aircraft soon after VJ day.

A formation of Barracudas carrying 1,600 lb torpedoes leaves Ronaldsway (the airfield is visible to the bottom right of the photograph). Bombing exercises took place between Douglas Head and Port Soderick or off the nearby Perwick Bay ranges. The torpedo element of the training programme was phased out during 1945.

As each practice torpedo or smoke bomb was dropped it would be cine-recorded from two points so that the pilot could monitor his progress and accuracy. Photography played an important role at the training station and a separate unit, responsible for all the photographs in this section, operated from the airfield. Members are seen here returning from a 'mission'. All the HMS *Urley* photographs shown here were taken by Charles Derek Shimmin.

A variety of other aircraft were used at the airfield. On 5 January 1945 a detachment of 722 Squadron moved to Ronaldsway to operate training flights for HMS *Valkyrie* at the Douglas Head radar station. They later moved to Andreas, but this photograph shows one of their Corsair Mk II's landing in September 1945.

A Grumman F6F Hellcat sits on the tarmac at Ronaldsway in August 1945. The Hellcat was famous for helping to win the air war in the Pacific, destroying more than 6,000 hostile aircraft, and was mass-produced to such a degree that 11,000 were delivered in two years. The Fleet Air Arm used Hellcats in Europe as well as the Far East, originally calling them 'Gannets' after their distinctive kinked square-tipped wings.

With three training units based on the Island there was inevitably a high accident rate, often resulting in the loss of crew as well as aircraft. The Fairey Barracudas seemed to be particularly unfortunate, and were involved in at least 30 accidents. Happily the incident shown in these two photographs passed without injury. On 28 September 1945 the Barracuda was taking off from Ronaldsway when the front of the aircraft suddenly burst into flames with smoke pouring from the engine cowlings. Sub Lt. P. J. Davis of 747 Squadron kept control and he and the crew escaped from the smouldering aircraft as it shuddered to a stop.

Following VJ day on 15 August 1945 there was a little more time available for ceremonial occasions, and these two photographs show an open day at Ronaldsway that October. The resident Barracudas are lined up for continuous takeoff.

Sunday morning divisions taking place under the eye of commanding officer Captain Shirley-Rollinson. HMS *Urley* was gradually run down and finally decommissioned on 14 January 1946.

Ronaldsway returned to civilian use and late in 1953 the length of the runway was increased by 200 yards to 1,600 yards, primarily to allow the use of an emerging new generation of larger aircraft. The Vickers Viscount 701 developed for British European Airways was foremost amongst these and after test and publicity visits a regular weekend service from Manchester started in 1955. This was the start of a long association between the Viscount and the Island at a time of rapid expansion in air travel.

SHIPPING

The *Mary Isabella*, the second Ramsey lifeboat of that name, arrived on 20 April 1896, towed from Whitehaven by the SS *Ellan Vannin*. Rigged like her predecessor with two lugs and a jib and rowing ten oars, the new boat was built to the latest designs and served for nineteen years seeing 48 service launches and saving 153 lives. A lifeboat day appeal is being made from the boat in this Edwardian T. H. Midwood photograph.

The Peel lifeboat the *Mayhew Medwin* and her crew are seen outside the old lifeboat house on the breakwater, beneath the walls of the castle. A self-righting, ten oared boat, the *Mayhew Medwin* required a crew of nine and served from 1897 until 1925 under coxswains John Wilson and Charles Cain, nephew of the Charles Cain of the famous St George rescue.

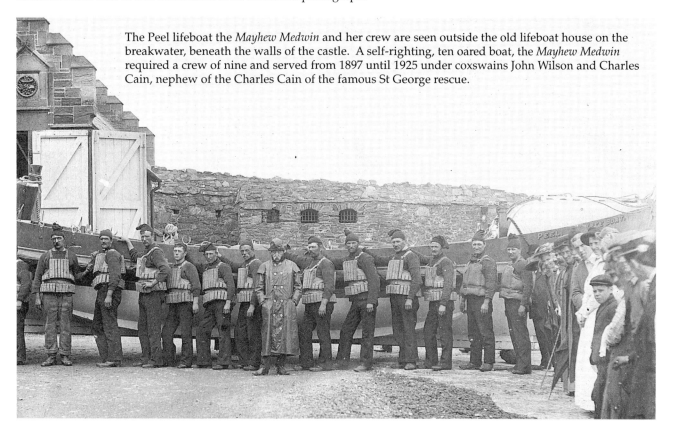

Port St Mary lifeboat station is the youngest on the Island, established in 1896 to cover the dangerous section of coast from Langness to the Calf of Man. The *James Stevens No. 1*, photographed by V. L. Swales, was the station's first lifeboat, serving until 1917 and saving 39 lives. Port St Mary boats no longer use the lifeboat house and are moored in the outer harbour instead.

When Coxswain Collister requested a larger boat for Port Erin in 1892 there was a danger of the station being moved to Port St Mary. A petition was successfully raised to keep the station, however, and the *William Sugden* went on to save nineteen lives during her 20 years of service. As can be seen, launching and recovering the lifeboat gave problems and a new slipway was built in the 1890s to improve conditions at the station.

Due to the numbers of holidaymakers that were visiting the town, Douglas had two lifeboat stations between 1887 and 1896: Douglas No. 1 on the promenade and Douglas No. 2 in the harbour. The promenade site was sold to the town commissioners in 1891 and a new boathouse was constructed near the Battery Pier with a steel slipway to allow easy launching of the boat. The new boathouse and slipway only became practical, however, when the swing bridge was constructed across the harbour in 1894–1895. Prior to that the Battery Pier would have been inaccessible from the lifeboatmen's homes in an emergency.

This photograph and the one above show the *Civil Service No. 6* of 1896 being launched down the new slipway in 1904. Prior to its launch the boat had to be dragged across the road over a series of skids, an operation that was sometimes delayed by the large crowds of onlookers who would gather to watch. As can be seen the boat entered the water at considerable speed. *Civil Service No. 6* served the station until 1924 when the current Douglas boathouse was completed to house the first motor lifeboat.

The Manx coast had a bad record for wrecks in the days of sail but even modern steam vessels were not immune from foundering. The Calf of Man is a particularly dangerous area and the SS *Irrawaddy* was fortunate to survive when she grounded below the disused lighthouses by the Stack in July 1905. Constructed by W. Denny & Bros. of Dumbarton only two years earlier, she belonged to the Burmah Steam Ship Co. Ltd. of Glasgow.

The steamship *Argo* of Glasgow ran off course and was wrecked on rocks at Meary Voar near Santon Head on 28 December 1905. The seas were heavy and the crew of fourteen stayed on board overnight after one of the ship's boats was destroyed. The Argo's second boat can be seen still in place here, and in the event the crew escaped by climbing down a ladder and scrambling to safety over the rocks. The first intimation of the wreck only came when they reached Santon railway station. Photographer W. Comery published postcards of many wrecks of the time.

The *Anna* of Castletown broke her back on the rocks between Dreswick Point and the Skerranes on the Langness peninsula on 14 April 1931. Sailing from Maryport with a cargo of coal, she ran aground during the night and became badly holed. The *Anna* was an auxiliary ketch built in 1895 and had a crew of four on board under Captain Faragher. They all reached shore safely in the ship's boat and the efforts seen here the next day managed to salvage part of the cargo.

The SS *Mayfield* of London was also carrying a cargo of coal, from Glasgow to Savona in Italy, when she hit a sharp reef to the north of Niarbyl Point in thick fog on 25 September 1909. Her distress signals were heard by nearby residents and the crew of 24 reached safety using the ship's boats. A large hole had been ripped in the vessel and she rapidly filled with water. All salvage efforts were quickly abandoned.

The *Kelburne* of 1891 was a local coasting steamer that
belonged to Gale and Co. for many years. Bound for
Liverpool on 28 November 1924, she ran into a southerly
gale and was unable to make the harbour when she turned
back for shelter. She was driven ashore against the
promenade wall in Chapel Bay below the Bay Hotel, and as
the tide went out the crew were able to walk to safety.
Heavy seas persisted over the next few days and by the
time the *Kelburne* was towed to Qualthrough's shipyard at
Castletown she was declared a total wreck and was sold for
breaking up.

The ST *Sulby* out of Fleetwood was more fortunate on 2
March 1912. Seen here ashore on the beach at Shellag Point
near Bride, the crew reboarded her the morning after the
incident and found her to be only slightly damaged. The
cargo of coal was unloaded and sold to local farmers and
the ship was then safely refloated.

The *Snaefell III* of 1910 must have been a rare visitor to Peel during her short life with the Steam Packet. The first of the company's vessels to be built at Cammell Laird's of Birkenhead, she was mainly intended for the Liverpool to Douglas winter service and was often seen on secondary routes during the summer. She was returning home from troop-carrying duties after a serious fire on board when she was torpedoed and sunk off Alexandria on 5 June 1918.

Destined to be the last paddle steamer in the fleet, the *Mona's Queen II* was built at Barrow in 1885. She operated the Fleetwood service until 1904, so this photograph of her leaving the Liverpool landing stage in May 1903 was unusual for the time. Her last passenger sailing was made on the Fleetwood to Douglas service on 31 August 1929, after which she was broken up at Port Glasgow.

A rare W. Comery postcard showing the ill-fated *Ellan Vannin* by the old Red Pier at Douglas. The *Ellan Vannin* was a unique vessel in the Steam Packet fleet, having started life in 1860 as an iron paddle steamer, the *Mona's Isle II*. Her conversion to a twin screw steamer took place at Barrow-in-Furness in 1882, and as the *Ellan Vannin* she enjoyed another 27 invaluable years of service before the fateful night of 3 December 1909 when she sank with all hands.

Prior to the outbreak of war in 1914, the number of passengers carried by the Steam Packet grew year by year, as did the number of steamers and the range of destinations served. By 1913 fourteen steamers were in service, and older vessels that usually served the seasonal routes could be laid up for the winter. The usual winter quarters were at Barrow, and no less than four Steam Packet vessels can be seen in this 1909 photograph.

The *Ben-my-Chree IV* was launched on 5 April 1927, the first of the five famous steamers to be built between the wars. The fashion of the time was for sumptuous carpeting and expensive wooden fittings, as shown in this view of the tea-room, complete with an impressive skylight. Walnut and mahogany were soon to give way to steel and synthetic materials, partly for reasons of economy but increasingly because of fire and safety precautions.

Conditions for third class passengers on deck were rather more basic, but many preferred the fresh air on a fine day, and certainly it was the friendliness and bracing sea air that attracted the faithful contract passengers and day-trippers through the years. This postcard dates from 1914 and it is only in recent years that the picture has changed significantly, with less freedom to roam on deck now being the order of the day.

Aboard Steamer, en route to Isle of Man.

The classic Steam Packet centenary vessel, the *Lady of Mann*, was built by Vickers–Armstrong of Barrow-in-Furness and launched on 4 March 1930. The ceremony was performed by the Duchess of Atholl, and the *Lady* entered service on the Fleetwood–Douglas route following sea trials on the Clyde. This Sankey's postcard shows that she originally had a black hull, only receiving her familiar pre-war white superstructure for the 1933 season. The *Lady of Mann*'s final passenger sailing was from Ardrossan to Douglas on 14 August 1971.

When a summer service to Ardrossan commenced in the 1890s it marked the end of direct sailings to the Clyde. The service operated in peacetime right through to 1985 when the link was a casualty of the Steam Packet's merger with Sealink. Postcard views of the vessels at Ardrossan are rarely seen; this 1930s example shows the *Mona's Queen III* of 1934 at the Winton Pier. The harbour was very exposed and difficult to enter in a gale but the summer service to the Isle of Man remained popular with Scottish holidaymakers.

The simultaneous building and launch of two new vessels – the *Fenella* and *Tynwald IV* at Vickers–Armstrong's yard in Barrow-in-Furness – was a new departure for the Steam Packet. Seen here on 16 December 1936, Miss J. Thin launched the *Fenella* and a Mrs Walford the *Tynwald*. Both vessels were intended for the winter service and differed very little in appearance. Sadly these similarities continued, and short careers with the company were followed by both vessels being lost on war service.

The *Rushen Castle* arrives at Douglas from Fleetwood in November 1945, a service she maintained throughout the war years. At the outbreak of war only the *Rushen Castle* and *Victoria* (later replaced by the *Snaefell IV*) had been left to maintain the passenger service, and matters really only improved during 1945 with the return from war service of *Mona's Isle IV* and the *Viking*. That year saw the withdrawal of the *Snaefell IV* after sterling service. The new ships under construction at the time were desperately needed by the Steam Packet to replace their ageing fleet.

The arrival of the Manx Electric Railway in Ramsey in 1899 effectively put an end to the regular daily pleasure sailings to and from Douglas and serving Laxey and the Dhoon en route. The *Manx Fairy*, seen here in Ramsey, and *Fairy Queen* (which belonged to the Mona Steam Ship Co. Ltd.) were the most famous vessels to operate these sailings. The twice-daily journeys took only 75 minutes, costing 1s 6d single or 2/- return, with special trips to Port St Mary also popular. The vagaries of the weather and the novelty of the new electric cars quickly made the coastal sailings uneconomic.

A more unusual visitor to Douglas was the Blackpool Passenger Steamboat Company's *Queen of the North*. Built in 1895 by Laird's of Birkenhead, the steam paddle steamer served with the company until the outbreak of war when, serving as a minesweeper, she was lost in 1917. Excursions from Blackpool's North Pier to Douglas were formerly very popular.

Laxey harbour was mainly used for the export of minerals from the Laxey mines and only came under the control of the Harbour Commissioners in 1890. The two piers could accommodate small coastal steamers such as the Cardiff-registered *Lochaber* seen here. Built by Scott and Sons of Bowling in 1901, she belonged to the Moorcroft Shipping Co. Ltd. The mines went into decline and finally closed in 1929, and pleasure boats have made up the majority of visiting craft to Laxey since then.

The condition of the harbour at Peel became a cause of ongoing concern. Not only was contaminated water being washed down from the mines at Foxdale, but mud and silt were a hazard to shipping and a cause of complaint from holidaymakers. D. W. Kee, a local photographer, shows the dredger *Orkney* with a second vessel, *Mallard*, in attendance deepening the channel of the harbour just prior to 1914.

The Island's history was once bound up with the fluctuating fortunes of the herring fisheries. By the 1870s the size of the herring boats had increased to a length of about 50 feet and a weight of 50 tons. In October herring were to be found in Douglas Bay; these were different fish from those caught off the Calf during the summer and were believed to come from the north-east. The fleet followed the fish, and most of the boats seen in this 1905 photograph of Douglas harbour are Peel registered.

Just a few years later and the nickeys and schooners in Port St Mary harbour have been joined by an increasing number of steam drifters. The vessel to the extreme left, CT96, is the *Honey Guide* of 1878, and was the last survivor of the old luggers when she was scrapped in 1928. Next to her is the *Zephyr*, bearing one of several Port St Mary boat names beginning with the letter 'Z'. The rapid decline in the local fishing industry meant that sadly nearly all the new steam vessels came from other parts of the British Isles, principally Scotland.

The biggest attraction of July 1907 was the visit of the First Division of the Channel Fleet to Douglas. Included were the cruisers HMS *Talbot* and *Juno* and six battleships: HMS *King Edward, Britannia, New Zealand, Hindustan, Swiftsure* and *Illustrious*. The *Illustrious* was only two years old and was the flagship of Rear Admiral Robert S. Lowry. Many shore-based attractions were arranged for the occasion and the Steam Packet took out several parties to view the fleet from the *Mona* and *Tynwald*.

The Douglas boatmen also reaped rich rewards conveying visitors to and from the ships. Indeed, one of the most noticeable changes to Douglas seafront today is the lack of the rich variety of pleasure boats that are to be seen in old photographs. Boats were rented from 6d to 1/- per hour, plus a gratuity if a man or boy was to accompany the boat. Fishing and trips to Port Soderick or Laxey were popular, but in the days of segregated bathing vessels were strictly forbidden from approaching the ladies' bathing machines. Boating parties were warned of the strong currents running near Douglas Head and much was said about the extortionate charges boatmen made for towing foolhardy trippers back into the harbour.

This Stafford Johns photograph shows the interest aroused by the visit of a squad of six submarines to Douglas. The H.21 class of coastal defence submarines dated from 1917 and were the fastest diving submarines in the Navy. They escaped without any wartime losses and after the war seven of the vessels formed the 3rd Flotilla serving with the Atlantic Fleet. From 1923 they were mainly used for training or testing new equipment. Of the submarines seen here, H29 foundered in HM Dockyard, Devonport in 1926 but H28 and H34 served right through the Second World War, only being sold off in 1944.

The speedboat *I'm Alone* was a familiar sight in Douglas during the 1930s. The boat was owned by a Mr Hawley who lived at 'Edale' on Victoria Road. He was involved in pilot training and died in a target drogue accident at Derbyhaven early in the war.

The 'Ben' boats of the Ramsey Steamship Company Ltd. have played an important part in the Manx economy since their first ship, the *Ben Veg* arrived in Ramsey in August 1914. The five-year-old, 366 ton *Jolly Basil* was purchased in 1924 and renamed the *Ben Jee*, serving the company until sold to United Molasses in 1933 and further renamed the *Morarill*. The Ben line survived the problems of the General Strike of 1926 and the Depression years that followed, with a fleet of seven vessels during this period.

Three losses followed in the 1930s: the *Ben Blanche*; *Ben Vooar*; and the *Ben Seyr* with the tragic loss of all hands in October 1938. The *Ben Ellan* of 1921 was bought in 1938 to bolster the fleet size, and the 274-ton coaster gave many years' service, finally being scrapped at Dublin in 1961. Two trucks can be seen on Ramsey's harbourside rail extension in this photograph.

BUSES

Douglas Corporation initially became involved in running public transport in 1902 when the horse trams and cable cars were acquired from the Tramways and Electric Power Company, which found itself in liquidation following the failure of Dumbell's Bank. The first motor buses were acquired in 1914, with vehicles being bought almost exclusively from the Tilling Stevens company up to 1930. This works photograph shows the very last vehicle obtained from them, a Tilling Stevens petrol-electrics with a Northern Counties 33 or 34 seater body. Given fleet number 40, the vehicle remained in service until 1945, as indeed did all the buses obtained from 1923 onwards.

This line-up at the Victoria Pier dates from 1926 and the complete fleet of the time seems to be represented, including the only double-decker, a Tilling Stevens TS3A. Nearest to the camera are a brand new Tilling Stevens TS6 and a Tilling Stevens TS17A from the previous year.

It was 1926 before buses were allowed on the promenades, and they took over the winter service from the horse trams the following year. Two very unusual Vulcan low-loaders were purchased in 1935, built in the style of the trams with a sliding roof and folding screens on the near side. They were only scrapped in 1957, although the roof and screens were permanently fixed soon after arrival. Route 10 displayed on the bus in this Robert Mack photograph was the Victoria Pier / Bucks Road / York Road service, once served by the cable cars.

It was only in 1949 that an Act was passed allowing Douglas Corporation buses to operate up to two miles beyond the borough's boundaries. This explains the strange termination point of this Tilling Stevens bus at Governor's Bridge on the Douglas boundary and well short of the population centre in Onchan. For many years route 32 operated to here from the Victoria Pier with routes 20 and 30 following a circular route taking in Quarter Bridge, St Ninian's, Governor's Bridge, Holiday Camp, Broadway, Promenades and back to Victoria Pier. Douglas Corporation bus services were finally absorbed in the new Isle of Man National Transport Ltd. in 1976.

Few bus services were provided outside Douglas before 1927, when fierce competition erupted between Manxland Bus Services Ltd., an offshoot of a Cumberland company and Manx Motors Ltd., a local consortium of rail and coach operators. The Isle of Man Railway Company broke away from Manx Motors the following year, operating its own fleet of newer and faster buses and soon taking over the fleets of the rival operators. Their initial purchases were Thornycroft BC vehicles with Hall Lewis two-doored bodies seating 28 passengers. This Thornycroft is seen in Castletown Square on a short service to Ballasalla, Rushen Abbey being a particular attraction for visitors at the time.

A rare glimpse of a Manxland Bus Services ADC 416A with a Hall Lewis body, seen in Ballure Road, Ramsey in August 1928. The railway company bought out Manxland's shares only six months later, and the ADC survived with them until as late as 1948. Initially fares had been comparatively high at 1/6 single from Douglas to Ramsey, but fierce price-cutting between rival operators led to the Cumberland company being forced out of business. Manxlands' vehicles often displayed a 'FULL' sign in their destination box, leaving crowds of eager passengers behind, and as their small buses only carried 20 or 28 passengers journeys quickly became uneconomic after the fares were reduced.

This Thornycroft BC was purchased new by the railway company in 1929 and survived until 1953 with Isle of Man Road Services. She is beautifully turned out here for a special occasion in the immediate pre-war period. These vintage buses still had to work all day services on the main routes even after the war.

The first new buses delivered to Isle of Man Road Services as opposed to the railway company were five Leyland LT5As with Northern Counties bodywork. No. 74 was delivered in 1934 and is seen here near the end of its working life behind the Ramsey garage in the Road Services livery of the early 1950s.

Douglas railway station was the favourite location for displaying new additions to the fleet. This photograph shows six Leyland Lion LT9s purchased in 1938, after which no more buses were added to the fleet for seven years. Each carried 28 passengers and all continued in service into the 1960s.

The batch of 32-seat Bedford OWBs with Duple bodywork that arrived on the Island in 1945 were the first new buses to be purchased for seven years. The vehicle seen here at the old Port Erin depot was given fleet number 28 and survived until 1966. The Bedfords were of semi-utility standard and as such were put to work mainly on secondary routes, although the need for replacements for the rest of the ageing fleet had become urgent by this time.

A second Bedford OWB from the same batch, this time sitting in an otherwise empty Ramsey shed. Older vehicles such as this were often to be seen in the north on the Maughold route or school services.

There appeared to be little hope of obtaining more single-deckers in 1945 (the British government only authorised the construction of double-deckers in the period immediately after the war), and the company took the unusual step of ordering twelve Leyland Titan double-deckers, although the law on the Island still limited vehicles operating outside Douglas to a maximum of 34 seats. Opposition to double-deckers centred on the tree-lopping that would be needed, but as the law did not specifically ban their use the company went ahead and introduced the first bus, which arrived with 22 of the 30 seats on the top deck barricaded off. Masterminded by manager A. H. Sheard, seen here beside the bus in question, this quickly illustrated the ridiculous nature of the law and the necessary legislation was soon passed to allow the general introduction of double-deckers early in the summer of 1947.

Above and opposite: Road Services' first double-decker was transported to the Island on 15 August 1946 on the Belfast, Mersey and Manchester Steamship Company's *Stormont*. These official Leyland Motors photographs were taken at Birkenhead docks. Given fleet number 3, the Titan remained in service until 1970.

Leyland Titans were to form the backbone of the service for the next thirty years. This sequence of photographs show the delivery of one of the eleven PD1s received in 1947. They followed eight months after the first experimental vehicle.

Opposite: GMN 780 being loaded on to the foredeck of the *King Orry* on 11 April 1947. This was the normal means of delivering vehicles, and relied on fine weather and a tide that brought the foredeck level with the pier roadway for unloading at Douglas.

A large batch of new Leyland Titan PD2/1s was ready for delivery in 1949 and Leyland Motors realised that it would be cheaper and less troublesome to arrange a special sailing. One of the Atlantic Steam Navigation Company's former tank landing vessels, the *Empire Gaelic*, was chartered to take fifteen of the buses to Douglas, then the largest shipment of double-deckers ever made from Britain.

Shipment took place from Preston Dock on Thursday 17 February 1949. The *Empire Gaelic* arrived at Douglas at 9.30 a.m., the first bus being hoisted off onto the south side of the King Edward Pier at 10.45 and the last at 2 p.m. The occasion attracted much local interest. Each bus arrived with a different destination displayed.

Four of the 1949 Titan PD2/1s parked behind the Ramsey garage, two with 'SCHOOLS SPECIAL' on their destination boards – a sure sign of approaching retirement. Three of them also seem to have local Ramsey depot numbers (R7, R4 and R5) in addition to their standard fleet numbers. All four vehicles were withdrawn between 1972 and 1974.

The complete delivery of eighteen Titans (three of the vehicles had to be delivered separately from those carried on the *Empire Gaelic*) was then lined up for publicity photographs at the Victoria Pier. Some of the buses continued in service until as late as 1974 and the second in the line-up (KMN 504) survives in perfect preserved state on the Island thanks to the efforts of David Bailey and fellow enthusiasts.

A Leyland Titan PD2/22 dating from 1956 decked out in full carnival regalia by the York Road depot. This vehicle, fleet number 94, was withdrawn in 1978.

CARS AND CARRIAGES

Car stands were to be found in all parts of Victorian Douglas and carriages of all kinds could be engaged with or without a driver. Maximum charges were fixed by law to protect holidaymakers and upwards of 800 vehicles were licensed to ply for hire, with many drivers coming from the mainland for the season. A trap would do for a small party, but visitors were still advised to engage a driver, not only for his local knowledge but also to free passengers from any responsibility in the event of an accident.

Larger parties would hire one of the big 'sociables' licensed to carry ten passengers. The 'Long Road to Ramsey' was the most popular whole-day trip, covering a total distance of about 40 miles and requiring a morning start at about 10 o'clock. The carriages left Douglas by the Peel Road, making stops at Glen Helen and Ramsey before returning via Laxey in time for dinner. The high-sided vehicles provided a good view above the hedges and also kept passengers well above the level of the dust from the unmade roads.

After 1918 motorised charabancs came into general use, with some adapted from lorries and others built specially and resembling very large cars with folding hoods. One of Alfred Clague's charabancs from Esplanade Motors is pictured here at Rushen Abbey in 1926. Photographer Arthur Hadley, who had the concession here, had to develop his postcard views extremely quickly to sell them to the visitors before they departed.

Famous manufacturers such as Leyland and Daimler produced versions of charabancs to seat between 23 and 33 passengers, the largest of which were needed here for an excursion from Cunningham Camp. Passenger doors were normally only fitted on the near side and solid tyres were only gradually replaced by pneumatic ones.

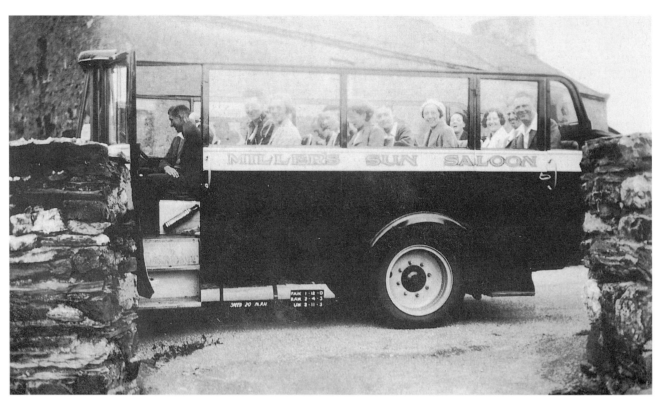

Holidaymakers were faced with a vast choice of operators and trips to take, although the days of the traditional open 'chara' came to an end as the vehicles gradually evolved into the enclosed saloon coaches of today. Miller's open-topped 'sun saloon' is on a short afternoon trip to Cregneash and the Sound in this 1934 picture. Miller's Motors' garage was in Station Road, Port St Mary.

In 1926 a trip in a hired car was still an opportunity to dress stylishly and impress the neighbours with a postcard. This photograph was taken outside T. H. Midwood's studio on Ramsey promenade. Even the busiest roads on the Island were impressively free from motor traffic right up to 1939.

The possession of motor transport could give a business a big advantage over its competitors, and Stacey's of Ridgeway Street, Douglas have produced a postcard to advertise their delivery service. As a bakery, they would have been able to supply local hotels and boarding houses much more easily with vans, as well as being able to serve previously unreachable out-of-town customers.

The 1890s had seen a massive increase in the popularity of the bicycle, but many of the older Manx roads were unsurfaced and very steep for cyclists, who also complained at the lack of signs indicating many of the lesser roads and pathways. Matters had improved by the 1930s, and a cycling holiday based at say Ramsey or Port St Mary offered many possibilities, with large groups of cyclists often taking part.

MOTOR CAR RACING

The story of motor car racing on the Island is well documented, principally by Robert Kelly in his book *TT Pioneers*. In fact the first race to take place in Mann, on 10–12 May 1904, was designated as a trial. This was in order to select the three cars and drivers who would represent England in the forthcoming international race for the Gordon Bennett Cup, which was to be held in France. Special laws had to be passed by the Manx parliament in order to close the appropriate roads, although in the event this process was not completed until just days before the trials were due to be held.

The success of the trials, combined with the advantage of roads that could easily be closed, led the authorities to agree to the holding of the first Tourist Trophy race in September 1905. Like the Gordon Bennett trials preceding it, the race covered the entire Island. There were 42 starters.

The opening and closing of numerous level crossings on the course caused innumerable problems, leading to modifications and the establishment in 1906 of the familiar TT course. TT motor car races were held on the Island in 1905–1908, 1914 and 1922. In the last of these years there were two races, both run together: the TT Race and the '1500' Trophy Race which was restricted to cars with an engine size of under a litre and a half.

It was to be eleven years before the Island was to see motor car racing again. In 1933 the RAC organised two races around the town of Douglas: the Mannin Beg, for cars up to 1500 cc, and the Mannin Moar for those over this limit. The 4.6 mile circuit was very demanding, involving eleven acute corners as well as innumerable lesser bends. Both races comprised 50 laps, giving a total length of 230 miles. Starting at the Villa Marina, the cars travelled along the promenade, then up Finch Road, Bucks Road, Woodbourne Road, and Governor Road, finally completing the circuit by going back down Summerhill to the promenade again.

Despite the fact that the authorities had been pressing for a renewal of motor car racing, the public's response to this was mixed. Many people living within the course resented being confined to their homes between 9 a.m. and 2 p.m. The closure of the foreshore also created a great deal of bad feeling, especially since the large notice announcing this closure was headed 'RAC', and not, as would have been more tactful, 'The Police'.

The Mannin Beg race of 1933 began at 9.30 a.m. on 12 July with fourteen cars taking part. These were made up of six MG Magnettes, four MG Midgets, two Rileys, a Frazer Nash and a Sullivan Special. Of these, only two completed the race.

The gruelling course took its toll, and by halfway the initial field had been reduced to just five cars, the other nine having nearly all dropped out because of mechanical failure. Very soon two more joined them, and of the remaining three it was likely that only one could finish the course within the time limit. The rules stipulated that, in order to finish the race, a driver must start his final lap no later than fifteen minutes after the winner has crossed the line. In addition, whatever happened, the roads must open at two o'clock. In the event, the leading driver, F. W. Dixon, cruised in 14 minutes 55 seconds ahead of D. K. Mansell (MG Midget), who was the only other driver to finish.

So the first Mannin Beg race ended with F. W. Dixon winning, but there was plenty of controversy! Ford and Baumer's MG Midget was flagged off after 49 laps having run out of time, but the RAC considered that theirs was such a splendid effort that they awarded them the money for third place anyway. There were howls of protest from some islanders. Naturally Ford and Baumer offered to return the money. Equally naturally the RAC refused to accept it!

It was against this backdrop that the Mannin Moar took place two days later. One of the many spoken criticisms

Automobile Club of Great Britain and Ireland.

THE INTERNATIONAL TOURIST TROPHY RACE,

ISLE OF MAN, 1905.

✳

ADMIT BEARER

TO THE CLUB'S ENCLOSURE, SELBORNE ROAD, ON THURSDAY, SEPTEMBER 14TH.

Tickets such as this one were only issued to the more privileged guests.

was, that if only two out of the fourteen cars taking part on Wednesday had managed to finish, would any finish in this race at all. There were nine cars taking part: five Bugattis, three Alfa–Romeos and an Invicta.

In the event, many of the fears proved ungrounded. The result was never a foregone conclusion and an exciting finish ended with the Hon. Brian Lewis as the winner, having travelled at an average speed of 64.23 m.p.h. Overall, three racing drivers finished within the permitted time limit, with T. E. Rose-Richards coming second with an average speed of 63.61 m.p.h. and G. E. T. Eyson third with an average of 63.05 m.p.h. One other driver was flagged off after 48 laps. Mechanical failure did not prove to be as much of a problem as it had been in the Mannin Beg, and only one driver retired because of it. The other four all crashed. The most spectacular crash was that of R. O. Shuttleworth in his Bugatti. At the end of 35 laps he attempted to pull up at the pits, realised that he had misjudged the manoeuvre, yanked on his handbrake which prompted the Bugatti to turn a complete somersault and crash into the pits. At least three pits were demolished and amid fuel churns, charts, funnels and other pit equipment, the legs of the pit personnel could be seen high in the air. Fortunately, no one was badly hurt. Shuttleworth took it all in his stride, his official reason for retiring being 'rear wheel tyre punctured'. His mechanic was not so sanguine, immediately changing out of his overalls and resigning on the spot.

The two races generated enough interest for them to be allowed to continue, and both took place again in 1934 and 1935, albeit with a slightly altered route. The new course started at the Palace and went up Broadway, turning at Bray Hill corner. It then extended past the Grandstand and Governor's Bridge, going back down Summerhill and proceeding along the promenade to the start again. There were now just three acute bends and a long straight of nearly one-and-a-half miles in the four-mile circuit. It was therefore not surprising that very high speeds were maintained during these years.

In 1936 only one race took place on the Island. It was renamed 'The International Car Race' and was restricted to cars with a capacity of up to 1500 cc. It also involved a completely different circuit, encompassing Glencrutchery Road, Ballanard Road, Crankybury, Hillberry Road, and Governor's Road. The race still, however, involved 50 laps and the length of the circuit remained steady at around four miles.

1937 saw the last motor car race to take place before the war, and once again it only included cars with a capacity of up to and including 1500 cc. The route, however, was changed again, as was the name of the race. 'The RAC Isle of Man Race', as it became, started at the Grandstand, went down Ballaquayle Road and Broadway, continued on to the promenade, went up King Edward's Road and Royal Avenue, along Onchan Main Road and Governor's Road and then on to Glencrutchery Road again. The length of the circuit and the number of laps required remained unchanged. The race was to start at 2.00 p.m. on Thursday 3 June. It was set at this time in order to enable spectators to travel from Liverpool to Douglas by the morning boat, see the race and return home that same evening. Special excursions were provided by the Steam Packet Company for 3/6 third class.

How many spectators took advantage of this offer is not known, but it is well documented that – as far as the weather was concerned – it was one of the worst days of the summer. It didn't stop raining throughout the race, although the conditions didn't deter the drivers. Five finished within the time limit, seven were flagged off and only three retired through mechanical failure. The winner was B. Bira in an ERA, covering the course in 2 hours, 45 minutes and 34 seconds at an average speed of 70.69 m.p.h.

Motor car racing was seen again on the Island in August 1947. The British Empire Trophy, which was run under the auspices of the British Racing Drivers Club, took place at Douglas because of a lack of suitable circuits in England. The winner was Bob Gerrard in an ERA at an average speed of 68.02 m.p.h.

Shell produced a series of very popular advertising postcards at the beginning of the last century. This is a rare example that was produced following the outcome of the 1908 race.

When you think of SPEED, think of "SHELL" MOTOR SPIRIT.

FOUR-INCH RACE, Sept. 24th, 1908.

HUTTON CAR WON ON "SHELL"

Only One Quality for Racing & General Use.

No. 66

This photograph of Sir Julian Orde's inspection tour of the proposed Gordon Bennett trials course was taken early in 1904. Automobile Club organising secretary Orde is driving, and next to him sits Lt. Governor Lord Raglan. In the rear are Colonel Freeth the Chief Constable and Deemster Kneen, while George Drinkwater, holder of the Island's first car registration number, 'MN1', stands to the left.

Landing cars at Douglas in 1904. This was the first time that a steamer on the Island had landed passengers on a Sabbath. During the trials the Island's car population was increased from two to over 50.

One of the components of the Gordon Bennett trials of 1904 was a speed test along the promenade at Douglas. It was during this that Clifford Earp crashed his car, with the above result, on the Villa Marina wall. Fortunately, no one was seriously hurt but the accident cost Earp his rightful place on the Gordon Bennett team.

Better days for Clifford Earp, seen here at the Napier headquarters at Douglas Bay Hotel; he was the winner of the 1905 Gordon Bennett trials.

The Hon. C. S. Rolls, driving a Wolseley, was one of the qualifiers for the 1905 Gordon Bennett Cup. This was Rolls' first appearance on the Island.

Unloading one of the two Star entrants for the 1905 trials at Douglas Quay. The brothers F. J. and F. R. Goodwin drove them.

John Hargreaves, driving a Napier, passes the start at Quarter Bridge at the 1905 trials.

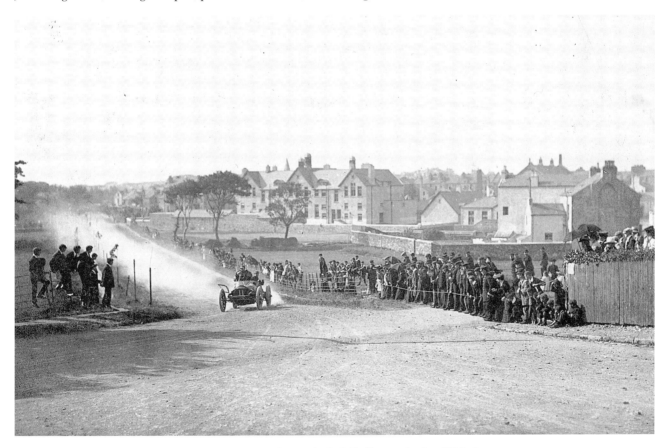

Crowds lining the route at Ramsey in the 1905 trials watch C. S. Rolls pass by in a Wolseley.

Car travelling at high speed over road treated with "Dustroyd"
Note dust raised from untreated portion.
Gordon-Bennett Motor Trials, I.O.M., 30th May, 1905.   R. S. Clare & Co., Ltd., Liverpool.

Dust was a constant hazard in the early days. This picture shows John Hargreaves driving on a section of road treated with something called 'Dustroyd', having presumably just passed through a dust storm in a section that was not thus coated.

WEIGHING IN "TOURIST TROPHY" RACE

Cars competing in the 1905 TT race had to adhere to strict conditions regarding weight. Here W. J. Warren's Speedwell car is being weighed. Because of the way the scales worked, the chassis had to be weighed separately, hence the lifting device. It took up to an hour for the judges to weigh one car and at the end of this all sorts of parts would be jettisoned to comply with the weight limits. The judges drew the line at the cardboard bonnet that the 14 h.p. Dixi substituted for the real thing when it was found to be 250 lb overweight.

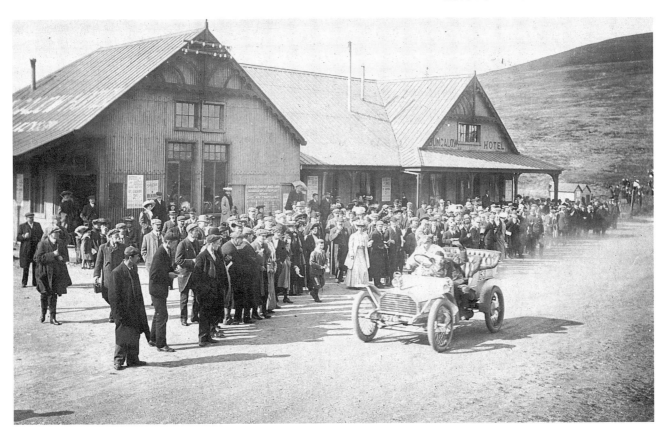

Winner of the first TT, John Napier, passes the Bungalow in his Arrol–Johnston. He covered the four laps of the course, a total distance of 208.5 miles, in 6 hours, 9 minutes and 14.6 seconds at an average speed of 33.9 m.p.h.

The officials and marshals who volunteer so much of their time are often the unsung heroes of the TT races. In the past many were stationed at remote and exposed parts of the course and could face a long and wet journey home in the days before motor transport became widespread. Here a somewhat overloaded Castletown Brewery lorry has found the strain too much after a long day at the car races.

Sulby Bridge suffered particularly from the depredations of the car racers and often displayed battle scars as a result. In 1906 Hugh McConnell's Bianchi crashed right through the stone wall, falling 10 feet onto the river bank below. Here R. H. Collier's West–Aster has been slightly luckier during practices for the 1907 event and awaits rescue, watched over by the long-suffering village constable. In the actual race Collier went out on the third lap, overturning on the Mountain road.

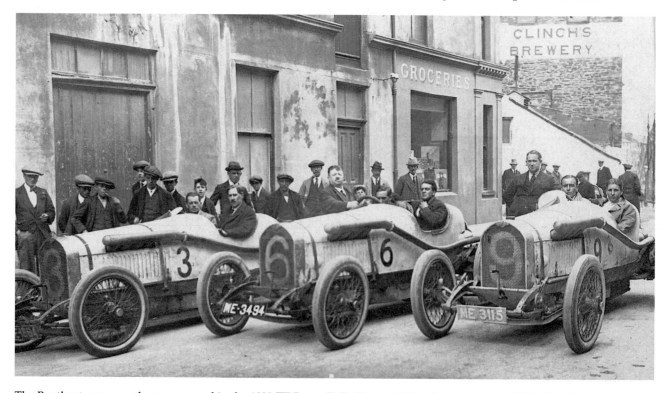

The Bentley team won the team award in the 1922 TT Race. F. C. Clement (No. 3) came second, W. D. Hawks (No. 6) was fifth and W. O. Bentley (No. 9) came fourth. Bentley lost his floorboards during the fifth lap and after that had nothing to support his legs but the pedals.

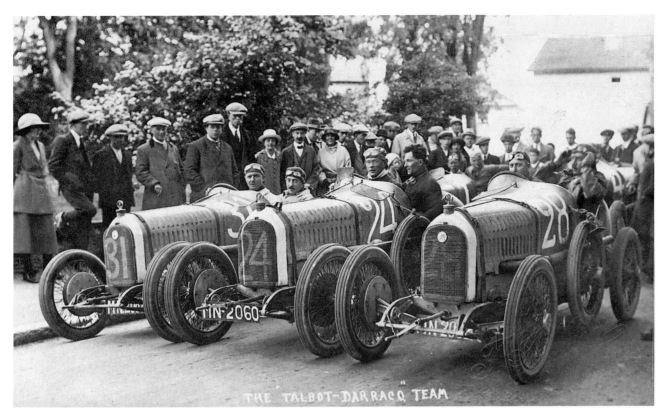

From left to right the drivers of these cars are A. Divo, Sir A. Lee Guinness, and J. Moriceau. Sir A. Lee Guinness and A. Divo came first and second respectively in the International '1500' Trophy Race of 1922.

The Bugatti team for the 1922 International '1500' Trophy Race. M. Maury (No. 27) came third, B. S. Marshall (No. 30) came sixth and P. de Vizcaya (No. 22) came fourth. The ambulance was not needed, despite the fact that in the evening after the race all the drivers were in considerable pain from the calcium chloride that had been used to stop the dust from rising and which had got into their eyes.

This picture gives some indication of the poor weather at Ramsey Hairpin as O. Payne (third in the 1922 TT) passes in his Vauxhall.

The start of the 1933 Mannin Beg race. At the line can be seen F. W. Dixon (No. 7) in a Riley, G. E. T. Eyston (No. 15) and H. C. Hamilton (No. 16) both in MG Magnettes.

F. W. Dixon (driving a Riley), winner of the 1933 Mannin Beg race, completed the course in 4 hours, 13 minutes, 35 seconds at an average speed of 54.41 m.p.h.

The start of the 1933 Mannin Moar. On the line from left to right are T. E. Rose-Richards, No. 9 (Bugatti); A. Brackenbury, No. 3 (Bugatti); G. E. T. Eyston, No. 11 (Alfa–Romeo); and B. Lewis, No. 6 (Alfa–Romeo).

The view immediately after the start of the Mannin Moar, after turning through Greenhill corner, with Brackenbury in the lead driving the Bugatti, and Eyston's Alfa–Romeo just behind, followed by the rest of the field.

The Hon. Brian Lewis won the Mannin Moar in 1933 covering the 230 miles in 3 hours, 34 minutes and 52 seconds at an average speed of 64.23 m.p.h.

The winner of the 1933 Mannin Moar with the drivers that came second and third.

Pat Fairfield came third in the 1937 race, and was just over a minute behind the winner. Here he is turning the corner at Broadway; the poor state of the road can be seen clearly.

The 10th British Empire Trophy race was held in Douglas in May 1948. Using a special 3.88 mile circuit on the outskirts of the town, it incorporated the motorcycle TT pits and grandstand. No. 20, F. R. Gerard, is rounding Cronk-ny-Mona, the far point of the course, prior to retiring after nine laps with a cracked brake backplate.

No. 36, Reg Parnell, passes No. 40, D. Hamilton, at the same point as shown in the previous picture. Both Masaratis also ultimately retired, Parnell after 35 of the 36 laps. He had been first or second throughout the race, the lead changing hands five times. The surprise winner was Geoffrey Ansell in an old B-type ERA, taking place in only the second race of his career. He had been well behind Parnell and his cousin Bob Ansell, another late retirement.

MOTORCYCLE RACING

On 31 May 1905 the Isle of Man achieved a unique double first when it held the first legalised road races for motorcycles ever to take place in the British Isles (it had, of course, held the first such race for motor cars the previous year). These were the elimination trials for the selection of the British team for the International Auto-Cycle Cup race. The proposed route was the same as that used for the motor car trials held on the Island. However, when a leading contender, T. F. Crundall, smashed his machine and broke his arm attempting to navigate the Ramsey Hairpin, the course was changed. The new route started at Quarterbridge, went southwards, then turned up through Foxdale before turning at Ballacraine to return to the start again. There were eighteen entrants for the race, eleven of whom turned up for the judges' inspection. Only seven finally made the start.

The race was set to begin at 3.00 a.m. Despite this early hour a significant number of people were to be found at all the best vantage points on the course. Because of a dense mist, the start was delayed, chiefly out of consideration for one of the competitors, H. A. Collier, who wore glasses. Such was the spirit of those pioneering days! At 3.30 a.m., with everything in order, the race was started by W. Hodgekinson, followed a minute later by C. R. Collier. Six of the competitors were soon speeding their way towards Ballasalla. The seventh, A. Barnes, turned up fifteen minutes late having been on a trial spin. Stating that the machine had never been better and making a few last minute repairs, he sped off to Ballasalla. He arrived about three hours later!

The race was due to finish before 8.00 a.m. so that the roads could be reopened at that time, and there was no set distance, save that the maximum number of laps allowed was seven. In the event the two finishers completed five laps. J. S. Campbell on a 6 h.p. Ariel came first in 4 hours, 9 minutes and 36 seconds, and H. A. Collier (despite his glasses) on a 6 h.p. Matchless came second in a time of 4 hours, 9 minutes and 52 seconds. A gap of only 16 seconds! Both had encountered enough serious incidents to affect the outcome of the race. The most dramatic of these was at the end of Campbell's first lap. When he was refuelling at Quarterbridge, petrol spilled all over his machine. On his departure, the machine caught fire and became a mass of flames. Technology was such in those days that it was a coat that saved the day, suffocating the flames. The two men went on to represent their country in the International Auto-Cycle Cup.

In 1907 the Island saw the first Motorcycle TT. The speed limit of 20 m.p.h. and legislation preventing road closure meant that the races couldn't be held in England, and the Island's authorities were only too happy to oblige and allow it to take place on Mann. The 1907 course started at St Johns and then proceeded through Ballacraine, Kirk Michael and Peel before returning to St Johns again – a lap distance of just under 16 miles and a total distance of around 158 miles. The event was divided into single cylinder and multi-cylinder machines, the races taking place concurrently. The first winner of the single cylinder event was C. R. Collier on a Matchless at an average speed of 38.22 m.p.h., although the result might have been different had the runner-up had pedals on his machine as well. The winner of the multi-cylinder event was H. Rem Fowler on a Norton at an average speed of 36.22 m.p.h. This event was the start of a series of TT races that have grown from strength to strength over the years and still take place today.

1905 international cup selection trials: the weigh-in at Quiggin & Co. Rope Works, Lake Road, Douglas on 29 May 1905. From left to right, the bikes and riders pictured are: No. 11, J. S. Campbell, 6 h.p. Ariel; No. 1, H. Hodgkinson, 6 h.p. Jap; No. 15, F. W. Barnes, 10 h.p. Barnes; No. 16, G. Wilton, 10 h.p. Barnes; No. 9, C B. Franklin, 6 h.p. Jap. Harry Collier is pictured leaning forward between Barnes and Wilton. (Michael Kelly collection.)

O. C. Godfrey won the senior TT race in 1911 on an Indian. This was the first year that the present course was used, and also the first year that races were classified as senior and junior. Godfrey also had the distinction of tying for second place in the 1914 senior race.

In the early days the competitors crowded round at the start listening to the instructions given by the course authorities.

The successful Indian team in the senior race of 1921 when F. W. Dixon finished second and H. le Vack came third. The other two competitors were N. H. Brown and H. R. Harveyson.

Here is the Coulson junior team of 1921 featuring D. S. Alexander, E. A. Jacob and H. Petty. Coulson only took part in the 1921 and 1922 races.

Behind the scenes: the Rudge garage of 1922.

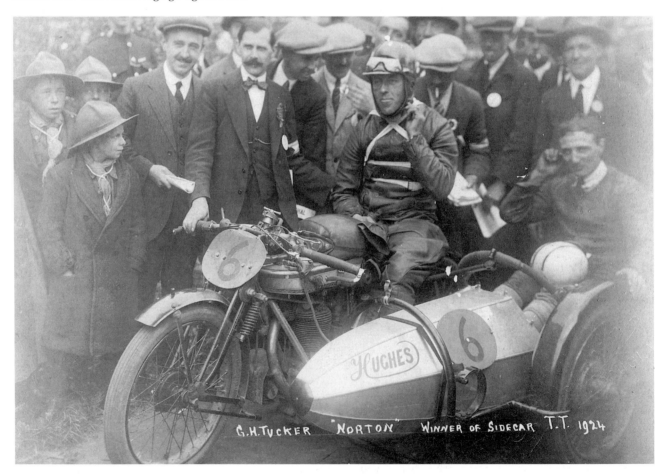

The first sidecar events were held in 1923. The only other years they were held before the war were 1924 and 1925. This picture shows the 1924 winner, G. H. Tucker. Boy scouts had helped in the races since 1910, performing such tasks as manning the position boards.

Jimmy Guthrie winning the 1934 junior on a Norton. He won a total of six TT races before his untimely death in the German Grand Prix of 1937. The Guthrie Memorial stands on the mountain road near the Cutting, a fitting memorial to one of Britain's greatest motorcyclists.

Another of the 'greats', the Dubliner Stanley Woods, photographed in 1938 on a Velocelte. He won the junior race, came second in the senior and second in the lightweight – just an ordinary year for Stanley. He rode in 37 TT races between 1922 and 1937, finished in 21, made eleven fastest or record laps and won ten races. In 1932, 1933 and 1935 he won two races in a week and was never placed lower than sixth. We are not told, but assume that the lady is Mrs Woods.

FURTHER READING

Boyd, J. I. C., *Isle of Man Railway*, 3 vols., 1993–1996.

Corkill, Adrian, *Dictionary of Shipwrecks of the Isle of Man 1740–1995*, 1995.

Goodwyn, Mike, *Manx Electric*, 1993.

Hendry, R. Preston and R. Powell-Hendry, *Manx Northern Railway*, 1980.

Kelly, Robert, *TT Pioneers*, 1996.

Kelly, Robert and Kniveton, G. N., *Sir William Hillary and the Isle of Man Lifeboat Stations*, 1994.

Kniveton, Gordon N., *Manx Aviation in War and Peace*, 1985.

Lloyd-Jones, David, *Manx Peacocks*, 1998.

Miles, Philip C., *Isle of Man Buses 1907–1988*, 1989.

Pearson, F. K., *Douglas Horse Tramway*, 1999.

Pearson, F. K., *Isle of Man Tramways*, 1970.

Shepherd, John, *Life and Times of the Steam Packet*, 1994.

This early view of the Douglas Southern Electric Tramway shows motor car No. 3 at Port Soderick with a trailer in tow. Four additional trailers, numbers 13–16, had been delivered in 1897; these seated 76 passengers and were similar to but lighter than the six originals. Until it was simplified in 1933, the livery was crimson and white, lined out in gold and white with trucks in black and rails and other fittings in brown.